UNTAMED

Greenville News   **Independent Mail**

Clemson head coach Dabo Swinney leaves the field with his wife Kathleen after the Tigers' 44-16 rout over the Crimson Tide. (Bart Boatwright/The Greenville News)

This book is available in quantity at special discounts for your group or organization.
For further information, contact:

Triumph Books LLC
814 North Franklin Street
Chicago, Illinois 60610
Phone: (312) 337-0747
www.triumphbooks.com

Printed in U.S.A.
ISBN: 978-1-62937-603-5

The Greenville News/Anderson Independent Mail
Katrice Hardy, VP / Executive Editor / South regional editor
Steve Bruss / Regional news director
Jim Rice / Sports editor
Chris McMahon / Sports planning editor
Photographers: Bart Boatwright, Ken Ruinard and Josh Morgan
Reporters: Scott Keepfer, Manie Robinson and Marcel Louis-Jacques

Content packaged by Mojo Media, Inc.
Joe Funk: Editor
Jason Hinman: Creative Director

Front cover photo by Ken Ruinard/Anderson Independent Mail
Back cover photo by Bart Boatwright/The Greenville News

CONTENTS

INTRODUCTION

By Jim Rice

Three years ago, we proudly published a book that recorded Clemson University's 2015 journey to the College Football Playoff Championship Game, *Return to Glory.*

Two years ago, we published *Clemson Crowned,* the cover of which featured a beaming Deshaun Watson clutching a fingerprint-smeared national championship trophy — the program's first in 35 seasons.

This season, we've published *Untamed,* our tribute to this amazing season.

The Greenville News and *Anderson Independent Mail* covered every moment of the 2018 season. We've packaged together the insightful observations of reporters Scott Keepfer, Manie Robinson and Marcel Louis-Jacques and the dynamic photography of Bart Boatwright, Ken Ruinard and Josh Morgan as the Clemson program became a two-time College Football Playoff champion and the first 15-0 team in FBS history.

Not that it was easy. This perfect season included drama early and late.

On the second weekend, The Tigers survived a late rally by Texas A&M to edge longtime Clemson nemesis Jimbo Fisher. Sixteen days later, with the Tigers 4-0 and ranked No. 2 in the country, coach Dabo Swinney made a change at quarterback, replacing senior second-year starter Kelly Bryant with heralded freshman Trevor Lawrence.

While that news rocked Tiger Nation, there was a sizeable aftershock two days later. Bryant announced he would transfer from Clemson rather than remain as a reserve.

Three days later, Lawrence left his first start because of a neck injury. Another freshman, Chase Brice, was asked to rally Clemson from a 16-7 deficit against Syracuse. Brice did, executing a remarkable pass and a gutsy run to keep the go-ahead drive alive.

That 27-23 win sparked one of the most dominant runs in Clemson football history. The Tigers won their next eight games by an average of 38 points and none by fewer than 20.

Then, as Clemson was preparing for its Cotton Bowl game against Notre Dame, there was more drama. Three Tigers, including star defensive tackle Dexter Lawrence, were suspended by the NCAA after testing positive for a banned performance-enhancing substance. Despite Lawrence's absence, the defensive line maintained its season-long dominance as the Tigers won their playoff games by 30 and 28 points for Clemson's second national championship in three seasons.

That leads us to this book. You'll find articles and photographs featuring a few familiar faces from *Return to Glory* and *Clemson Crowned,* but mostly you'll find the new faces who took the spotlight in this second championship run.

That's what may be most memorable about the 2018 season. The characters who highlighted the chapters of *Glory* and *Crowned* were much the same. But almost all had moved on to the NFL or other

No stranger to the national spotlight, Clemson nonetheless put together a season for the ages, becoming the first 15-0 team in over a century. (Ken Ruinard/Anderson Independent Mail)

professional careers when the Tigers assembled this past August for preseason camp.

In addition to the new quarterback, a running back and a trio of receivers emerged as headline-grabbers for the offense, which averaged 248 yards rushing and 279 yards passing per game.

The defense was perhaps even more impressive, led by three linemen who were projected as high NFL draft picks after the 2017 season but delayed that opportunity for this one. The Tigers limited opponents to an average of 285.7 yards per game, fifth-fewest in the 129-team FBS, and a best-in-the-nation 13.1 points per game.

Their achievements are documented on the pages that follow. We hope you'll enjoy smearing your fingerprints over every one.

Jim Rice
Content Coach/Sports

Above: Coach Dabo Swinney holds the College Football National Championship trophy, accompanied by defensive lineman Christian Wilkins, left, and cornerback Trayvon Mullen. Opposite: Travis Etienne (9) breaks free from Alabama defensive back Jared Mayden to score during the first quarter of the College Football Playoff title game in Santa Clara. (Bart Boatwright/The Greenville News)

COLLEGE FOOTBALL PLAYOFF NATIONAL CHAMPIONSHIP

Clemson 44, Alabama 16
January 7, 2019 | Santa Clara, California

ALL WINS

Tigers dominate Crimson Tide for 15-0 season, national championship
By Scott Keepfer

Trevor Lawrence finally had his "freshman moment."

He handled it like an NFL veteran.

Lawrence guided Clemson to touchdowns on five consecutive possessions bridging the first and second halves as the Tigers pulled away for a 44-16 victory Monday night over No. 1 and previously undefeated Alabama and claimed their second national championship in three years.

Lawrence, who unseated incumbent Kelly Bryant as Clemson's starting quarterback in the season's fifth game, showed why in front of a Levi's Stadium crowd of 74,814, completing 20 of 32 passes for 347 yards with three touchdowns.

Lawrence, who became the first freshman starting quarterback since Oklahoma's Jamelle Holieway in 1985 to lead his team to a national title, was named the Offensive Player of the Game.

Clemson junior cornerback Trayvon Mullen was selected Defensive Player of the Game.

"Our guys had a clear vision of how they wanted this to go tonight," Clemson coach Dabo Swinney said. "It was a complete performance all the way through.

"There was a lot of talk about 'best ever' all year long. Well, we proved it. This team won 13 games by 20 points or more, led by an amazing group of seniors."

Monday's result certainly had to be a just reward for

players such as Christian Wilkins, Austin Bryant, Clelin Ferrell, Mitch Hyatt and Kendall Joseph, all of whom opted to pass on the NFL Draft last year to play another round with the Tigers.

They stamped their careers emphatically, dealing Alabama its most lopsided defeat ever under coach Nick Saban.

Meanwhile, Lawrence outshined heralded Alabama quarterback Tua Tagovailoa, who completed 22 of 34 passes for 295 yards with two scores but was intercepted twice, including a pick 6 for a touchdown on the Crimson Tide's third play of the game.

Clemson freshman wide receiver Justyn Ross, an Alabama native who had the best game of his career in a 30-3 romp against Notre Dame last week in the Cotton Bowl, followed that performance up with a six-reception, 153-yard, one-touchdown night that included multiple one-handed catches.

The Tigers had to log a lot of miles to accomplish their goal this time around, traveling more than 7,000 miles — first to Dallas, then to Santa Clara — to claim the third national title in school history, joining the 1981 and 2016 teams in completing the quest.

Clemson's convincing victory against Alabama reaffirmed that the Crimson Tide does indeed have company atop the college football world.

On Monday night, the Tigers elbowed their way to

Quarterback Trevor Lawrence runs for a first down during the fourth quarter of the College Football Playoff National Championship game. Lawrence easily outworked Alabama's Tua Tagovailoa in the 44-16 victory. (Ken Ruinard/Anderson Independent Mail)

the pinnacle once again, toppling Alabama for the second time in three years and in doing so becoming the first team in the modern era to win 15 games in a season.

Clemson improved to 5-2 in the College Football Playoffs during the past four years, and the Tigers' senior class matched Alabama with 55 victories and two national titles in that time span.

Swinney proclaimed almost 10 years ago that the next decade would the best in school history.

He was right. The Tigers have 103 wins this decade, joining Alabama and Ohio State as the only teams in the country with 100 wins or more.

With a 2019 season remaining this decade, there could be more to come, particularly for a team whose key playmakers are all underclassmen.

Sophomore running back Travis Etienne rushed for 86 yards and scored three touchdowns against the Crimson Tide, and sophomore wide receiver Tee Higgins had three catches for 81 yards and another score.

Opposite: Clelin Ferrell and defensive lineman Christian Wilkins (42) bring down Tua Tagovailoa, who struggled against the formidable Clemson defense. (Bart Boatwright/The Greenville News) Above: Trayvon Mullen (1) returns a second-quarter interception, cheered on by Coach Dabo Swinney. (Ken Ruinard/Anderson Independent Mail)

Alabama pulled ahead 16-14 early in the second quarter, but it was all Clemson from there. Lawrence and the Tigers scored on five consecutive possessions to take command. Etienne scored on a 1-yard run with 11:38 left in the half to give Clemson the lead for good, 21-16, and then Clemson scored again following an interception that Mullen returned 46 yards.

Lawrence tossed a 5-yard shovel pass to Etienne for a score that put the Tigers ahead 28-16, and the Tigers capped the half by driving 61 yards in eight plays for a 36-yard Greg Huegel field goal that provided a 31-16 halftime cushion.

Clemson put the game away by scoring quickly after thwarting a fake field goal attempt on fourth down — one of three fourth-down stops the Clemson defense made.

Lawrence tossed a 26-yard touchdown pass to Ross for a 36-16 lead and then hit Higgins with a 5-yard

Opposite: Clemson defensive lineman Dexter Lawrence (second from left) celebrates with teammate Nyles Pinckney (44) after Pinckney tackled Alabama's Mac Jones to stop a fake field goal attempt in the third quarter. (Ken Ruinard/Anderson Independent Mail) Above: Wide receiver Amari Rodgers (3) acknowledges his teammates following a first-down reception during the second quarter. (Bart Boatwright/The Greenville News)

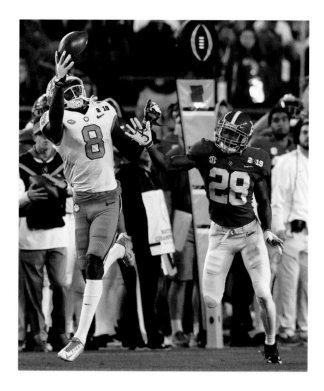

touchdown pass with 21 seconds left in the third quarter for a commanding 44-16 advantage.

Clemson amassed 482 yards while Alabama had 443 yards. Clemson's defense had seven tackles for loss, including two sacks, and held the Crimson Tide's leading rusher — Najee Harris — to 59 yards.

Clemson has not allowed an opposing running back to rush for more than 100 yards in 20 consecutive games dating back to the 2017 season.

Clemson, which entered the game as a 5½-point underdog, denied Saban his sixth national title at Alabama.

"I'm so happy for our team, our fans, our administration, our former players that love the paw," Swinney said. "There ain't never been a 15-0 team. And I know we're not supposed to be here — we're just little ol' Clemson — and I'm not supposed to be here, but we are and I am. How about them Tigers?

"We beat Notre Dame and Alabama and we left no doubt." ∎

Above: Wide receiver Justyn Ross makes a one-handed catch past Alabama defensive back Josh Jobe, one of his six catches in a huge performance for the Tigers. Opposite: Head coach Dabo Swinney (right) celebrates with defensive coordinator Brent Venables after Clemson stopped Alabama on fourth down in the third quarter. Venables' defense held the Crimson Tide to just 16 points. (Bart Boatwright/The Greenville News)

Running back Travis Etienne (9) scores against Alabama during the first quarter, one of his three touchdowns in the dominant win. (Bart Boatwright/ The Greenville News)

TOP OF THE HILL

After tough climb, Clemson enjoys view from the mountaintop

By Manie Robinson

One does not need to reach the top of the mountain to enjoy the view.

Clemson conquered an arduous 15-step climb. The Tigers encountered several hazards along the steep incline. There was no room for error. A single slip could have sent the Tigers tumbling.

Yet, while inching up the perilous path, the Tigers savored each step. There was a lesson in every triumph. There was insight in every stumble. There was joy in every day.

The Tigers kept their footing after the fourth game, when quarterback Kelly Bryant was demoted in favor of freshman Trevor Lawrence and transferred from the program.

The Tigers marched through tears a week later when former running back C.J. Fuller unexpectedly died.

Clemson did not lose a step when it lost Dexter Lawrence, a central cog in its defensive line, after a failed drug test.

The Tigers pulled close through prosperity. They pulled even closer through adversity. At each step up the mountain, they stopped, looked proudly over the land they covered, took a deep breath and headed back up the hill.

On Monday night, Clemson finally completed the climb. The Tigers marched past Alabama to claim the College Football Playoff National Championship.

Clemson scaled this mountain for the second time in three years. The second pass to the peak was no less difficult, but according to Clemson coach Dabo Swinney, it was more joyful.

"In '15, it was a blur," Swinney said, alluding to Clemson's first run to the CFP national championship game in 2015. "I don't even really remember it. It was very new."

Swinney said Clemson's return to the title game in 2016 was more of a business trip.

"It was almost like that whole season everybody just wanted to hit fast forward," Swinney said. "Like OK, can we just get there? We know where we're going. Can we just get there?

"It doesn't work that way. That was a little more of a grind. But once we got there, they were ready, and we won the game."

Swinney said, this year, this team recognized that the process was just as important as the product.

"This has been a very joyful season is the best way I can say it," Swinney said. "A lot of times, it's felt like this team kind of wanted to hit pause, and I do think that they've enjoyed the journey. I do think this senior group has savored every moment along the way. They haven't looked ahead."

And now, there is nothing ahead of them. Not another step. Not another team.

Clemson can stand proudly at the same elevation with Alabama. The Crimson Tide entered Levi's Stadium

Clemson cornerback Trayvon Mullen (1) holds the College Football National Championship trophy as defensive lineman Christian Wilkins (42) celebrates after the Tigers defeated Alabama 44-16 at Levi's Stadium. (Bart Boatwright/The Greenville News)

with a longer lineage, a bigger brand and a larger share of the national acclaim.

Yet, Monday night, Clemson was assured and convicted in its scheme. Alabama resorted to desperate gimmicks and fakes.

Clemson exhibited a dazzling array of playmakers. Alabama flashed infrequently only on Clemson miscues.

Alabama quarterback Tua Tagovailoa entered the game as the lauded composer. But Lawrence was the brilliant virtuoso. Tagovailoa was flustered under Clemson's immense pressure. Lawrence stood tall in the pocket, took bone-rattling hits and delivered dimes off his back foot.

Tagovailoa completed three of his first six passes on third down. He gained 48 yards. Lawrence completed eight of 12 third-down passes for 240 yards and two touchdowns.

Alabama averaged 47.7 points per game through its previous 14 contests. Clemson limited the Tide to merely three points after the first quarter.

Clemson was the aggressor. Clemson was the instigator. Clemson was the better team.

And Clemson is once again the national champion.

"It's just an amazing moment," Swinney said. "Having done this before, you enjoy this moment. We're certainly going to enjoy it, but at the end of the day, it's really more of an appreciation of the journey here, what we went through to get here, the grind, the struggles."

The Tigers can look proudly over the land they covered, take a deep breath, and if Swinney has his way, they'll head back down the mountain and prepare for another climb.

"Can't wait to get back started Friday," Swinney said, "and see if we can figure out a way to go do it again." ∎

Defensive lineman Austin Bryant sheds a tear after the overwhelming Clemson victory, handing Alabama coach Nick Saban his worst loss in his remarkable tenure with the Crimson Tide. (Ken Ruinard/Anderson Independent Mail)

A.J. Terrell's (8) pick-six set the tone early for Clemson and foreshadowed the incredible performance to come by the Tigers. (Ken Ruinard/ Anderson Independent Mail)

Clemson 48, Furman 7

September 1, 2018 | Clemson, South Carolina

FRESH START

Clemson's freshman talent shines in season-opening romp against Furman

By Scott Keepfer

Clemson's defense is heavily populated by veterans while Clemson's offense is laden with younger talent.

Both were in strong evidence in Saturday afternoon's 48-7 pasting of Furman in the Tigers' season opener at Memorial Stadium, but it was the instant impact of the youngsters that caught the eye of both coaches and the 80,048 fans on hand as Clemson successfully launched its bid for a fourth consecutive College Football Playoff berth.

Freshmen or sophomores accounted for four of the Tigers' six touchdowns.

Clemson's leading passer and leading rusher were both freshmen, and six of the 11 receivers who caught a pass are underclassmen.

"I was watching the wideouts every play," co-offensive coordinator Jeff Scott said. "It was good to see lot of guys make some plays, especially some of those freshmen."

Rookie quarterback Trevor Lawrence entered the game with 13:04 left in the first half and had an immediate impact, guiding the Tigers to scores on three consecutive drives, the second of which covered 95 yards and included the 6-foot-6 freshman from Cartersville, Georgia, completing three of six passes for 66 yards.

"That was the drive that changed the game," Scott said. "We had that drive that was 95 yards and another that was 92. On that 92-yard drive we had several freshmen making plays, and that was good to see."

"When you have a talented team like we have and are still able to play young guys and let freshmen get opportunities speaks a lot to Coach (Dabo) Swinney and what he believes in."

Lawrence's first career touchdown pass was a 6-yard dart to Diondre Overton early in the second quarter. Lawrence later added touchdown passes to a pair of fellow freshmen — wide receiver Justyn Ross (15 yards) and tight end Braden Galloway (9 yards).

Scott said the scoring grab by Ross reminded him of Sammy Watkins, circa 2011.

"He's off to a good start," Scott said. "Just like Sammy, who scored in his first game."

Freshman Derion Kendrick also came up big with a 38-yard reception in the third quarter.

Lawrence wound up completing nine of 15 attempts for 137 yards and three touchdowns; starter Kelly Bryant was 10-of-16 for 127 yards and one score, which would seem to indicate that we'll likely see both get substantial playing time once again next Saturday at Texas A&M.

Freshman running back Lyn-J Dixon was as advertised, leading the Tigers' ground attack with 89 yards, including the longest run of the day, a 61-yard effort.

And freshman kicker B.T. Potter, who earned a reputation for a big leg at Rock Hill's South Pointe High, booted six of his seven kickoffs for touchbacks, with the other resulting in a fair catch.

"Freshmen are different than they were a few years ago," Scott said. "It makes you feel good about our future." ∎

Quarterback Trevor Lawrence reacts after throwing his first career touchdown to wide receiver Diondre Overton against Furman during the second quarter of the season-opening win. (Ken Ruinard/Anderson Independent Mail)

The Clemson defense suffocated the Paladins' offense all game, limiting them to 163 total yards. (Bart Boatwright/The Greenville News)

Clemson 28, Texas A&M 26
September 8, 2018 | College Station, Texas

NO. 2 TIGERS SURVIVE A THRILLER

Wallace seals victory with interception on two-point conversion in final minute

By Scott Keepfer

Last week, Clemson coach Dabo Swinney said he hoped his team would have a better result than it did during his first trip to Texas A&M's Kyle Field — a 27-6 defeat in 2004.

He got it Saturday night.

Barely.

The No. 2 Tigers' 28-26 victory appeared to produce more questions than answers — most notably the performance of a porous secondary that enabled Texas A&M to wage a late comeback and put the Tigers squarely on the ropes.

"Hat's off to Texas A&M," Swinney said. "Their team played with incredible heart. If you let a team hang around, you get in a dog fight, and that's exactly what happened."

The Aggies' big dog was sophomore quarterback Kellen Mond, who looked like an All-American against Clemson's defense, passing for 430 yards with three touchdowns and rushing for 33 yards.

His idol is former Clemson and current Houston Texans star Deshaun Watson, and Mond accomplished a fairly accurate portrayal of his hero Saturday night.

"When I watched him on tape, I said this kid has a lot of moxie and is going to be a tough out," Swinney said.

Suffice to say that Clemson's secondary deficiencies will need to be addressed immediately, particularly if the Tigers have intentions of reaching the College Football Playoff for a fourth consecutive year.

Clemson improved to 2-0, but it took K'Von Wallace's interception in the end zone of Mond's two-point conversion pass with 46 seconds to go to seal the deal for the Tigers.

"This was like an opener all over again," Swinney said. "This is the type of game that I think you can really grow from."

The growth will need to start immediately.

The Aggies' receivers were as wide open as the Texas horizon on more occasions than defensive coordinator Brent Venables would care to recall, but rest assured he'll be making adjustments, most likely beginning on the plane ride home.

Given what Mond was able to accomplish, Clemson's secondary will need to regroup. The Tigers will face several talented quarterbacks in Atlantic Coast Conference play this season, most of whom possess more impressive credentials than Mond, or at least they did going into Saturday's game.

That group would include Syracuse's Eric Dungey, Wake Forest's Sam Hartman and N.C. State's Ryan Finley. Mond has shown them a blueprint, and suddenly that looms as the Tigers' primary concern.

Clemson defensive back K'Von Wallace clutches the ball in the end zone after intercepting Texas A&M's two-point conversion late in the fourth quarter to seal the win. Wallace also forced a fumble out of the back of the Clemson end zone for a touchback late in the game to help thwart the Aggies. (Bart Boatwright/The Greenville News)

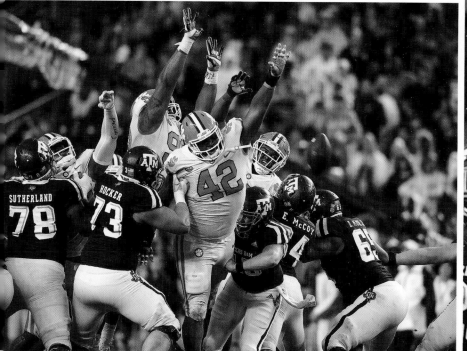

Other takeaways from Saturday's nail-biter:

• Did the Tigers' two-quarterback system work again?

Yes, for the most part. But even though freshman quarterback Trevor Lawrence entered the game and tossed a 64-yard touchdown pass to Tee Higgins on his first play, his next five series netted a total of two first downs.

Bryant was the player the coaches entrusted down the stretch, leading each of Clemson's final six possessions.

• Despite repeated setbacks, the Tigers had answers in almost every instance. That's a good sign for developing this team's mettle.

Such bounce-back was particularly strategic when Texas A&M had a quick, two-play scoring drive for a touchdown late in the third quarter that cut Clemson's lead to 21-13. Led by Bryant, who completed four of five passes for 62 yards on a 75-yard scoring drive, the Tigers carried a 15-point lead into the fourth quarter and would need each of them.

Above: Clemson defensive lineman Christian Wilkins (42) blocks a Texas A&M field goal during the second quarter of the two-point win. Opposite: Clemson wide receiver Tee Higgins scores past Texas A&M defensive back Charles Oliver for one of his three catches for 123 yards in the game. (Bart Boatwright/The Greenville News)

• The moment wasn't too big for most of the Tigers' youthful playmakers and certainly not for sophomore wide receiver Tee Higgins. Higgins' highlight-worthy reception on Lawrence's first pass was a prime example, as was a 64-yard catch-and-run by fellow sophomore Amari Rodgers that set up another score.

• The defensive line kept pressure on Mond all night, amassing 10 tackles for loss, including four sacks. Particularly effective were the Tigers' ends: Clelin Ferrell had three tackles for loss, including two sacks, and Austin Bryant flashed his relentlessness and undoubtedly caught NFL scouts' eyes with two tackles for loss and a quarterback hurry.

• Clemson's interior defense and linebackers were solid, too. The Aggies were held to 71 yards rushing — 2.2 yards per carry — one week after they rushed for 503 yards against Northwestern State. Also, massive defensive tackle Dexter Lawrence blocked a 50-yard field goal attempt in the second quarter. ■

Above: Clemson quarterback Kelly Bryant carries the ball against Texas A&M. He finished with 15 carries for 54 yards and a touchdown. Opposite: Clemson wide receiver Diondre Overton points to Texas A&M defensive back Donovan Wilson after catching a touchdown in the win. (Bart Boatwright/The Greenville News)

Clemson 38, Georgia Southern 7
September 15, 2018 | Clemson, South Carolina

STUFFING THE OPTION

Clemson turns back another option offense, moves to 3-0
By Scott Keepfer

Clemson prepared itself for a trip to Georgia Tech next week by successfully stuffing an option-oriented offense Saturday for the second time in three weeks.

The Tigers held run-heavy Georgia Southern to 246.5 yards below its rushing average, which effectively paved the way for a 38-7 victory in front of 79,844 sun-drenched fans at Memorial Stadium.

That exposure to the option, which is employed so heavily by Georgia Tech, could pay dividends as the Tigers prepare for their first Atlantic Coast Conference game of the season.

"The option offense isn't easy to defend because every option team isn't the same," Clemson defensive end Austin Bryant said. "It's a challenge each time you play those option teams. But we were locked in in our preparation this week, and I think it showed."

Bryant had two sacks, as did fellow defensive end Clelin Ferrell, and 28 players made at least one tackle, leaving defensive coordinator Brent Venables feeling positive.

"I was pleased with our effort and our attitude … it wouldn't have made a difference if we were playing the Denver Broncos or Mary Poppins State," Venables said.

Mary Poppins State has suddenly emerged as a popular fictional opponent for the Tigers, but the reality is that No. 2 Clemson is off to a 3-0 start for a fourth consecutive season and for the seventh time in eight years. The Tigers are 46-4 in their past 50 games dating back to the 2014 season.

Some other takeaways from Saturday:

Kelly Bryant's status: One point of concern that emerged regarded starting quarterback Kelly Bryant, who left the game late in the first half and did not return. He landed hard with his chest on the ball after being tackled on a run with just less than seven minutes left.

Bryant, who completed seven of 10 passes for 68 yards and rushed six times for 27 yards in the first half, returned to the sideline at the outset of the fourth quarter and told Swinney he was "OK."

"As of right now, we're told it's just a chest bruise and we feel he's going to be OK," co-offensive coordinator Jeff Scott said.

Committing turnovers: Clemson didn't have a turnover in the first two games of the season but began playing catch-up in that regard against Georgia Southern. Quarterbacks

Clemson wide receiver Justyn Ross eludes Georgia Southern safety Kenderick Duncan Jr. on his way to scoring during the second quarter at Clemson's Memorial Stadium. Ross had three catches for 103 yards in the comfortable win. (Bart Boatwright/The Greenville News)

Bryant and Trevor Lawrence each threw interceptions, and running back Adam Choice lost a fumble.

"We were really good through the first two games," Scott said. "We had some good drives going, but turnovers are drive killers. We wanted to get 80 plays offensively and we ended up with 77, and we had three turnovers. Each of those turnovers cost you a minimum of three plays right there."

Justyn Ross is an emerging star: Although just a freshman, the 6-foot-4 wide receiver continued to flash his skills. He had a 57-yard touchdown reception that included a couple of nifty moves to help him go the distance and finished with three catches for 103 yards.

"He's one of those guys that when he gets his opportunity, he makes the play," Scott said. "He's really coming into his own. We really challenged him this week in learning the playbook and understanding everything about his position. And he went out and made some plays."

Sharing the wealth: Ross wasn't the only receiver to have a good day. Quarterbacks Bryant, Lawrence and Chase Brice completed passes to 14 receivers.

"It's nice," said Lawrence, who completed 12 of 19 passes for 194 yards. "Everyone on the field is a great player, so you can go anywhere with the ball at any time. It's really good to have that freedom." ∎

Clemson running back Travis Etienne (9) carries the ball against Georgia Southern. He finished the day with 16 carries for 162 yards with two touchdowns. (Bart Boatwright/The Greenville News)

16
QUARTERBACK
TREVOR LAWRENCE

What defines Clemson QB? His faith and hometown

By Marcel Louis-Jacques | September 21, 2018

Cartersville High School football coach Joey King gets a call from high school sports website MaxPreps.com after the 2014 season; his quarterback, Trevor Lawrence, has been selected its National Freshman of the Year. King immediately calls Lawrence, who is at home playing video games, to let him know.

"I said look, you got the MaxPreps National Freshman of the Year, I just wanted to call and tell you that," King recalls. "And he said, 'OK coach, that's real cool, can I call you back in about five minutes? I've got to finish this game' … He did, he called me back later but his demeanor didn't change. It was just, 'Yeah, that's pretty neat' and went on. But that's just him."

Clemson quarterback Trevor Lawrence might be one of the biggest things to hit football in recent memory. The freshman was one of 247Sports.com's highest-rated recruits ever coming out of Cartersville High School, drawing attention from every college coach with a pulse.

Already labeled a generational talent, Lawrence arrived at Clemson in January under an enormous spotlight, but ask anyone who knows him to describe him and one word will routinely pop up — calm.

As it turns out, even when 100,000 people are watching, it's easy to stay grounded when you know your next move won't define you.

"It's kind of always been my personality. Football is important to me, obviously, but it's not my life," Lawrence said. "It's not the biggest thing in my life. I would say, my faith is. I would say knowing who I am outside of that, so I just know no matter how big the situation is, it won't define me."

Most of the football world sees Lawrence as a phenomenal quarterback, a future first-round NFL draft pick. Mention his name in Cartersville, Georgia, however, and make a list of everyone who brings up his talent before his character. You won't need much room.

His demeanor, while God-given, was fostered by King's program at Cartersville High School. His statement that football doesn't define him reflects the mindset King instills in all his players — that they're more than the game they're playing.

"We do a lot of different stuff to where the kids understand that their value doesn't just come from their performance on the field," King said. "We've got 120

Clemson quarterback Trevor Lawrence took the starting job as a true freshman and ran with it, leading the Tigers to their second national championship in three years. (Bart Boatwright/The Greenville News)

total kids in the program — well, 11 are going to play at a time. So if their success, or who they think they are, is based on the results of what happens on that field out there, then we're failing as coaches."

King's message is not uncommon among coaches, especially at the youth and collegiate levels. Like anything you try to teach a teenager, it may not always stick.

It did in Lawrence's case. He doesn't put much stock into what media outlets may anoint him; in his words, he prefers to identify with what Christ says he is.

That confidence aided him during his recruitment, during spring and fall camps at Clemson and during the Tigers' first three games of the season. It helped him develop as Cartersville's leader — by example, early on, and vocally toward the end of his career.

"That was something that he embraced more and more each year, especially his junior and senior year," King said. "You saw that it was his team and his role was to be the leader of the team. Just loving on the guys and serving them, which is what good leaders do."

* * *

Cartersville High School's principal Shelley Tierce joins her staff in the school's main office, where the conversation centers around the community's admiration for Lawrence. She offers her favorite story, which took place on a football field but had little to do with the game itself.

One of Cartersville's offensive lineman's shoes became untied during a game, and his bulky knee brace made it difficult for him to kneel down to tie it. Noticing the issue, the 6-foot-6 Lawrence dropped to a knee and tied it for him.

The Lawrence family attends church a stone's throw away from Cartersville High School at Tabernacle Baptist Church and has done so for most of Don Hattaway's 16 years as its pastor.

If he didn't see him play Friday night, Hattaway knew Trevor and his family would be in the congregation Sunday. Their attendance was as reliable as one of the passes Trevor tossed on the field less than a mile away.

"That's always been impressive to me," he said. "It just underscores their desire to raise their children in the Lord. To watch that through the years has been a great encouragement to a lot of people, I believe."

Amanda and Jeremy Lawrence taught their son to nurture his faith in God and raised him to be compassionate and kind — traits Hattaway says aren't always synonymous with star athletes.

But once again, while he remains a star in Cartersville, its residents are seemingly more fond of Trevor Lawrence the person than Trevor Lawrence the quarterback.

"Trevor's always been very polite, hard-working — he excels at everything he does. Always very respectful," Hattaway said. "I'm not at all surprised at his success on the field; he has certainly the physical ability and the mental aptitude to be an incredible leader. Beyond that, I think his character is more inspiring to me. It's not just what he does on the field, it's how he carries himself. I know he has a concern for people; he always takes time to speak to people, even little kids.

"A lot of people look up to him because of his position, but he's always taken time to show kindness to everyone."

* * *

Jacob Burson eagerly tells his favorite Trevor Lawrence story from the Orphan Aid, Liberia office in Cartersville. Cartersville High is ahead big during Lawrence's freshman season. He completes a long pass to wide receiver Terrius Callahan, who nearly scores before he's stripped of the ball at the 3-yard line. With his team on its opponent's 5-yard line later in the game, Lawrence rolls right out of the pocket and passes to a diving Callahan for a touchdown. It is an impressive play, but Burson can't help but notice Lawrence

Trevor Lawrence was the MaxPreps National Freshman of the Year in high school in 2014 and came to Clemson with huge expectations — nothing new for the likely future first-round NFL draft pick. (Bart Boatwright/The Greenville News)

has seemingly missed a wide-open tight end, Miller Forristall, who called for the ball right in front of him.

After the game, Burson spoke to Cartersville's offensive coordinator about the play. The coach had asked Lawrence whether he'd seen Forristall before throwing to Callahan.

"Yeah, I saw him," Lawrence replied. "But Cally needed that one more, Coach."

Daryl Roberts isn't one to ignore the Lord's instructions. When the opportunity to join a mission trip to Liberia arose in July 2008, he took it. He didn't know why God wanted him there, but he knew it was where he was supposed to be.

While in Liberia, Roberts conveyed his passion for helping orphans to a local missionary, who then directed him to a nearby orphanage in a state of disrepair.

Roberts said the orphanage was "a disaster," with 67 malnourished children living under an unreliable roof. Roberts knew he couldn't return to his bed in Cartersville until these children were taken care of.

God had shown him his purpose.

"I had complete clarity at that point — this is why I was here," he said. "There was absolutely no doubt."

With the help of his wife, Chrissy, Roberts secured enough funds to leave the children with some food before he left Liberia. They started Orphan Aid, Liberia, a nonprofit organization that feeds, medicates and educates orphans in the West African nation.

Ten years after its founding, Orphan Aid, Liberia serves 1,027 kids, operating with a staff located in both Cartersville and Liberia. Roberts said he and his staff have never missed a food drop nor an opportunity to provide medical care. Of course, neither feat would be possible without money, which Orphan Aid, Liberia sought through donations and T-shirt sales.

Luckily, he said, the support from Cartersville has been "phenomenal."

"They've bought thousands of these shirts. They see the purpose behind it, they know where the money's going," Roberts said. "These shirts are magical shirts because you pay for a shirt, you get a shirt, but it turns into food 5,000 miles away. They truly are beautiful."

The money from the organization's T-shirt sales provides meals for orphans in Liberia and has been a smashing success. Roberts said the organization orderd its 28,000th shirt in September and expects to serve its 1 millionth meal some time in the next two months.

The shirts' success drove Orphan Aid, Liberia to develop a "Gameday Line" in colors from schools in the area, like Georgia, Alabama and Clemson.

That's where Trevor Lawrence came in.

Lawrence noticed of the organization's kiosks at church, bought one of its shirts and even modeled the Clemson shirt with Orphan Aid, Liberia's motto — LOVE — emblazoned across the chest.

"It doesn't work when people don't buy (the shirts), but when they do it's super, super impactful," Roberts said. "Trevor's definitely been a help to us and we're grateful for that."

* * *

Joey King accompanies Trevor Lawrence to San Antonio in January 2018 for the U.S. Army All-American Bowl. A pair of players he says are currently making a name for themselves at the collegiate level approach him to ask how Lawrence, the nation's No. 1 recruit, built a social media presence of more than 100,000 Instagram followers.

"They were just talking to me and said, 'Coach, what does Trevor do to get all of his followers? What does he do? We're trying to get our brand up,'" King said. "I'm like, 'Man look, he couldn't care less about all that stuff.'

"That blew their mind. Realistically, he couldn't care less about how many people follow him."

Jack Howell has spent the past 25 years around the Cartersville High football program. The former president of the Touchdown Club is the team's current public address announcer and the "voice of the Hurricanes" on the radio when the team plays away from home.

Trevor Lawrence's talent on the field is outshined only by his stellar reputation off the field, particularly in his hometown of Cartersville, Georgia. (Bart Boatwright/The Greenville News)

He's seen Division I players come and go, including running back Ronnie Brown, who played at Auburn and was the second overall pick of the 2005 NFL draft. He sees some similarities between the two players' recruitments, with Lawrence's standing out in a noticeable way.

"Ronnie got a lot of local consideration, whereas Trevor was nationwide," Howell said, mentioning that fans came from as far as Ohio to watch him play. "I mean, over here at spring practice his junior year, we had 100 colleges come through spring practice. I'm not talking small colleges, I'm talking Notre Dame, USC, Arizona, Oregon."

Howell credited King, Amanda and Jeremy Lawrence for Trevor Lawrence's ability to handle the immense attention — the former for developing Lawrence's character and the latter for instilling it in the first place.

"He can talk to anybody, it doesn't matter who you are. A big sportscaster down to a neighbor next door, or just somebody off the street," Howell said. "He's able to relate to them, talk to them. His parents are the same way. A lot of time when you get a ball player that's getting that much notoriety, what his parents will do sometimes is take it and run with it. But his parents were level-headed with it, they kept it down to a minimum.

"It was just a neat thing to watch — a unique thing."

* * *

Taller than most with long blonde hair, it's difficult for Lawrence to avoid attention, especially for a player who plays a prolific position as well as he does. But despite his disdain for the spotlight, he maintained a level of accessibility you wouldn't expect from arguably the most recognizable person in town.

"He doesn't love the attention. That's not him at all," King said. "He wants to get out of there as quick as he can, but he would always take time if people were lined up until we had to run him off. Because he would've stayed out there forever.

"I think one night they were standing out there and they started to cut the lights off."

King's grandfather passed away a few years before Lawrence left Cartersville, but the coach chose to remain with his team as it prepared for a regional playoff game. It's what his grandfather would've wanted, King said, and his dedication didn't go unnoticed.

Cartersville won the game, and while King gave a postgame interview, Lawrence weaved through the crowd to let King know he appreciated him.

"Even in high school, (after a game, people) swarmed him. Kids lining up and we'd have to rush him to get out of there," he said. "But wanted to be sure that he found me and he hugged me before he got out of there. That was pretty cool."

King and Lawrence still talk almost every Thursday, rarely about football but instead how the teenager is doing mentally, how he's doing in school and how his walk with the Lord is going. If they do talk football, it's generally Lawrence asking about the team, specifically Cartersville's starting quarterback Tee Webb, who guided the Hurricanes to a 4-0 start to the 2018 season.

Lawrence speaks to Webb whenever he can, offering his former understudy pointers and confidence boosts over the phone. King says Webb, a three-star recruit on 247Sports.com with offers from Kansas State and Louisville, will be a Division I quarterback due in large part to his talent and the time he spent studying Lawrence.

"Emulating success," King called it; a common habit among successful people.

"That makes a lot of people successful," King said, "when they do what successful people do. I think it says a lot about both of them, but to see Trevor encourage Tee through that process … that says a lot about Trevor, too."

On the field, Lawrence's game speaks for itself; he may not speak at length about his character off it, but he doesn't need to.

Cartersville will do that for him. ◼

Trevor Lawrence laughs with head coach Dabo Swinney during pregame before playing Boston College. A big part of Lawrence's success comes from his calm and loose demeanor on the field. (Bart Boatwright/The Greenville News)

Clemson 49, Georgia Tech 21
September 22, 2018 | Atlanta, Georgia

MESSAGE SENT

Lawrence throws four touchdown passes in ACC opener

By Scott Keepfer

Georgia Tech entered Saturday's game against Clemson ranked No. 1 in the nation in rushing offense.

Suffice to say the Yellow Jackets may not be No. 1 on Sunday.

And we can only guess who the Tigers' No. 1 quarterback will be come Monday.

"We're not going to set the depth chart in the postgame press conference," Clemson coach Dabo Swinney said Saturday evening.

Perhaps not, but the writing could be on the wall.

Freshman quarterback Trevor Lawrence, the backup to starter Kelly Bryant through the Tigers' first four games, made a statement in his home state by tossing four touchdown passes to power the second-ranked Tigers to a 49-21 victory against Georgia Tech at Bobby Dodd Stadium.

Lawrence impressed the home folks in his first game as a collegian in his native Georgia, completing 13 of 18 passes for 176 yards. He has a team-leading nine touchdown passes this season.

Clemson's offense got off to a sluggish start, managing only one first down during its first two possessions but came to life when Lawrence entered the game early in the second quarter.

Lawrence capped a seven-play, 74-yard drive with a 17-yard across-the-body throw to Hunter Renfrow for a touchdown, then two plays later connected with fellow freshman Justyn Ross for a 53-yard touchdown. He was intercepted on the Tigers' next possession, leading to Georgia Tech's first touchdown, but responded by guiding the Tigers 64 yards in 12 plays for another score courtesy of a short shuffle pass to Travis Etienne.

Lawrence re-entered the game late but stayed just long enough to toss a fourth touchdown pass, this time Tee Higgins.

Georgia Tech coach Paul Johnson's assessment of Lawrence?

"He's a good player," Johnson said. "He's very accurate and he's a good athlete."

Perhaps we'll find out just how good during the remaining eight games of the season.

The rest of the afternoon was left to Clemson's suffocating defense. Georgia Tech entered the game leading the nation in rushing at 392.7 yards per game but was held in check for a fourth straight year by the Tigers' defense. Clemson has allowed the Yellow Jackets to rush for an average of 127.5 yards per game in their

Trevor Lawrence had a huge game in the win against Georgia Tech, throwing for four touchdowns and helping rout the Yellow Jackets. (Bart Boatwright/The Greenville News)

current four-game winning streak against Tech.

On Saturday, Tech managed 146 yards rushing — 246.7 below its average.

The Tigers recorded 10 tackles for loss, matching their season high, including four sacks, and Georgia Tech completed only three of eight passes for 57 yards.

"I was really pleased with how disruptive we were," Swinney said.

The defense set the tone early by recording the Tigers' first touchdown when defensive end Clelin Ferrell pounced on a loose ball in the end zone for a score with 3:42 left in the first quarter.

Clemson's defensive effort bodes well considering the team's next two opponents — Syracuse and Wake Forest — rely heavily on the run. Syracuse, which rushed for 162 yards against the Tigers in last year's upset victory, and Wake Forest both rank among the Top 20 rushing teams nationally this season.

"They embarrassed us last year," Swinney said of the Orange.

Clemson's running backs turned in their best effort of the season. Etienne rushed for 122 yards on 11 carries, his second consecutive 100-yard game, and pushed his per carry average to a gaudy 8.5 yards.

Sophomore Tavien Feaster also got in on the fun, rushing eight times for a season-high 75 yards, including a 27-yard touchdown, and the top four running backs each received at least five carries.

Bottom line? Clemson outrushed Georgia Tech 248-146, marking only the 19th time the Yellow Jackets have been outrushed in 133 games under Johnson.

"A lot of good things in the run game," Swinney said. "We had some explosive plays." ■

Justyn Ross glides in for the 53-yard touchdown on a pass from Trevor Lawrence. (Bart Boatwright/The Greenville News)

LAWRENCE GETS STARTING NOD

Freshman sensation overtakes Bryant for lead role

By Scott Keepfer | September 24, 2018

Trevor's the man.

Well, at least for Saturday's game against Syracuse.

Clemson coach Dabo Swinney announced Monday morning that freshman Trevor Lawrence will get the starting nod at quarterback when the Tigers play host to the unbeaten Orange in a noon game at Memorial Stadium.

"You've got to award production," Clemson co-offensive coordinator Tony Elliott said Monday.

Graduate Kelly Bryant had started each of the last 18 games for Clemson, including the first four games of this season.

But an ineffective performance by Bryant in Saturday's win at Georgia Tech and a four-touchdown performance by Lawrence precipitated a change in the depth chart.

Bryant completed 6 of 10 passes for 56 yards and a touchdown and rushed four times for five yards on Saturday. Lawrence entered the game early in the second quarter and guided Clemson to five touchdowns in six possessions.

The 6-foot-6 rookie from Cartersville, Georgia, completed 13 of 18 passes for 176 yards and four touchdowns.

"He was very productive with his opportunity," Swinney said Sunday evening. "He managed the pocket well and he was very patient when he got outside the pocket. He was accurate. He did a lot of good things for sure.

"There's definitely still room for improvement. He's a work in progress every week, but it was definitely his best game. He was very poised. The game has slowed down for him and he's making good decisions with the ball."

Lawrence has thrown for 600 yards in four games while completing 65 percent of his passes. He also has passed for a team-leading nine touchdowns.

He becomes the first freshman to start at quarterback for Clemson since Deshaun Watson was named the starter over Cole Stoudt for the fourth game of the 2014 season. Watson passed for a school-record six touchdowns in that first start, a 50-35 win against North Carolina.

Bryant, who guided Clemson to a 12-2 record and a third consecutive College Football Playoff berth last season, has completed 66.7 percent of his passes for 461 yards and two scores this season. He's also rushed for 130 yards and two touchdowns on 30 carries.

"They both have played well and done a lot for us," Elliott said. "It just came down to rewarding productivity. You look at his (Lawrence's) opportunities and he's taken advantage of them.

"Kelly didn't do anything wrong; it's just a situation where he's been in a game, he's been productive and to be fair to competition — just like we do at every position — coach decided to name him the starter for this game. Again, it's not a lifetime contract. He's got to prove it in practice and in the next game." ∎

The future came quickly for the Clemson football program, as freshman Trevor Lawrence was named the starting quarterback leading up to the fifth game of the season. (Bart Boatwright/The Greenville News)

BRYANT ANNOUNCES HE WILL TRANSFER

Quarterback makes decision after falling behind Lawrence on depth chart

By Manie Robinson | September 26, 2018

Kelly Bryant started the past 18 games for Clemson. He will start his next game for another school.

On Sunday, coach Dabo Swinney informed Bryant that he was no longer the starting quarterback. On Tuesday, Bryant informed Swinney that he will transfer.

Under new NCAA redshirt guidelines, by leaving Clemson now, Bryant can salvage his final year of eligibility. He has not decided where he will spend it.

"I feel like it's what's best for me and my future," Bryant said in an exclusive interview with The Greenville News. "I was just going to control what I could control and try to make the most of my opportunity, but at the end of the day, I just don't feel like I've gotten a fair shot."

Bryant, a senior from Calhoun Falls, started the first four games of the season but split series with freshman Trevor Lawrence.

Bryant completed 66 percent of his pass attempts and averaged 8.6 yards per throw. Lawrence completed 63.9 percent of his attempts and averaged 9.8 yards per throw. Bryant amassed 610 yards of total offense. Lawrence compiled 631.

Bryant directed eight scoring drives. He scored four touchdowns himself. Lawrence steered 15 scoring drives. He threw nine touchdowns, including four Saturday at Georgia Tech.

Swinney asserted that the quarterback rotation would continue, but he never affirmed that Bryant would always take the first turn. Swinney portrayed the switch as a reward for Lawrence, not a punishment for Bryant.

"They asked me how I felt about it," Bryant said, recalling his meeting with Swinney. "I was like, 'I'm not discrediting Trevor. He's doing everything asked of him, but on my side of it, I feel like I haven't done anything to not be the starter. I've been here. I've waited my turn. I've done everything y'all have asked me to do, plus more.'

"I've never been a distraction. I've never been in trouble with anything. To me, it was kind of a slap in the face."

Bryant signed with Clemson in 2014 after an All-State career at Wren High School. He appeared in 12 games through his first two seasons at Clemson, as he bided time behind Deshaun Watson.

Bryant seized the starting role in 2017. He became the third native South Carolinian to start at quarterback for Clemson since 2000.

He led the Tigers to a Palmetto Bowl victory, an Atlantic Coast Conference championship and an appearance in the College Football Playoff. Bryant accrued 4,300 yards of total offense and 32 touchdowns through 30 career games.

He compiled a 16-2 record as a starter.

"I've been with this senior class for four years. Seeing how much we built and poured into this program, it's tough to walk away from it," Bryant said. "But at the same time, I've got to do what's best for me. And I feel like this is the best situation for me."

The demotion fell at a favorable point on the schedule for Bryant. The NCAA loosened its restrictions on redshirting this season. Players can now appear in a maximum of four games without sacrificing a year of eligibility.

If Bryant played a single snap against Syracuse, his college career would be over in January. By withdrawing from the remainder of the season, he will be eligible to play immediately at another program next year. ∎

Senior Kelly Bryant made the tough decision of transferring out of Clemson after losing the starting quarterback job to Trevor Lawrence. (Ken Ruinard/Anderson Independent Mail)

Clemson 27, Syracuse 23
September 29, 2018 | Clemson, South Carolina

CLEMSON WINCES BUT WINS

Worst-case scenario unfolds as Lawrence injured before Brice rescues Tigers

By Manie Robinson

Fans cheered as Clemson quarterback Trevor Lawrence escaped pressure and sped around the edge. They exclaimed as he tipped along the sideline. They gasped as he collided with Syracuse safety Evan Foster.

They groaned as he rolled slowly to his back. The loudest silence swept across Death Valley as fans feared the worst.

Clemson coach Dabo Swinney is a meticulous man. He scrutinizes every detail in the configuration, aesthetics and messaging of his program. When he decided that now was the appropriate time to promote Lawrence to starting quarterback over senior Kelly Bryant, he had to assess all possible outcomes.

Best-case scenario, Bryant would accept the demotion and gladly embrace a relief role. That did not happen. He decided to transfer, and Swinney watched the worst-case scenario unfold on the 45-yard line.

Lawrence suffered an apparent head injury with approximately five minutes remaining in the second quarter. He did not return.

Swinney could not call Kelly Bryant from the bullpen. If he assessed all outcomes, Swinney cannot call Bryant's departure or Lawrence's injury unintended consequences of his decision. He was forced to confront that decision directly.

He also was forced to confront his longstanding assertion that Clemson could win the Atlantic Coast Conference championship with former third-string quarterback Chase Brice.

Swinney thrust Brice into his first meaningful playing time. Brice completed three of his first five passes for four yards and an interception. But he steadied enough to direct a 13-play, 94-yard, game-winning touchdown drive that included a gorgeous 20-yard pass for a fourth-down conversion.

"Game on the line and he throws a strike," Swinney said. "Obviously was disappointed that Trevor got hurt, but long-term, I think all things work together for the good.

"I said coming into the season, we had three quarterbacks that I thought we could win the league with. We've got two."

Lawrence's abrupt absence and Brice's early struggles induced Clemson's offensive coordinators to filter the offense through bruising running back Travis Etienne. Even with Syracuse stacking 12 in the box, Etienne amassed 203 yards and three touchdowns on 27 carries.

Clemson has continuously pressed snooze on his workload, but he is the eardrum-splitting alarm clock that woke Clemson from its worst nightmare.

Bryant would have smoothed the transition after

Trevor Lawrence is checked on by staff after getting hit during the second quarter of Clemson's close win over Syracuse. His injury in his first game as the starter and after Kelly Bryant announced he was transferring was a seemingly worst-case scenario for Clemson. (Ken Ruinard/Anderson Independent Mail)

Lawrence suffered the injury. He would have eased the nerves of everyone in Clemson orange and shredded Syracuse's porous defense. His experience would have rescued the Tigers.

Just like it did Sept. 8 at Texas A&M.

Swinney inserted Lawrence to start the second half that night, but the offense sputtered through two three-and-outs. Swinney reinserted Bryant. He led two touchdown drives and salvaged a victory.

Bryant did not denounce Lawrence's impressive performances through the first four games, which included nine touchdown passes. Nevertheless, Bryant believed his own performances, added to his 16-2 record as a starter, were enough to retain his starting role.

Swinney disagreed.

An impassioned discussion ensued. Bryant left Clemson heartbroken. He agonized over his decision to transfer, but he ultimately decided to move on.

Clemson had to move on as well.

Above: Clemson wide receiver Hunter Renfrow lunges for the catch, one of three for 45 yards in the win. (Josh Morgan/The Greenville News) Opposite: Clemson backup quarterback Chase Brice runs for 17 yards and a first down. Brice started slowly after replacing an injured Trevor Lawrence but made big plays down the stretch and helped Clemson to a gutty victory. (Ken Ruinard/ Anderson Independent Mail)

"Everything in your life is about how you respond," Swinney said. "It's not about what happens great in your life or challenging in your life. It's how you respond. I've never been more proud of a team in all my life.

"I saw a team grow up. I saw a team stand up and have each other's back. And just not quit."

Swinney asserted that he did not anticipate Bryant would leave, and he did not agree with the reaction. But he also asserted that he would make the decision again.

That certainty seemed faulty as Lawrence rolled in agony. Even before the injury, the offense had produced merely seven points and did not look drastically different than it would have with Bryant.

A resilient defense, a determined running back and an overwhelmed foe saved Swinney from a weekend of second-guessing, perhaps not in his own mind but from the same analysts, fans and media members who praised his decision and condemned Bryant earlier this week.

Some other fans delighted in the irony, which is inexplicably repulsive. No one should ever savor satisfaction from a young man's injury. The combative nature of our discourse instantly lines people on opposite sides of the 'net and encourages them to hurl diatribes at each other.

This situation must be evaluated with nuance. More than one thing can be true. More than one person can be right. More than one person can be hurt.

With Lawrence's status still uncertain, both Bryant's detractors and supporters wondered if his decision could be reversed. He is still enrolled at Clemson. Technically, he could change his mind and rejoin the team.

But Bryant reversing his decision would not make Swinney reverse his. Lawrence is injured. He is not broken. Once Lawrence returns, Bryant would be in the same situation. Swinney would be forced to confront another assertion — that he would make the same decision again.

Besides, Clemson will continue to thrive in the ACC, even in Lawrence's absence. Brice earned the trust of his team and the respect of his doubters. He was thrust into a nightmare situation, and he produced a dream outcome. ∎

Travis Etienne carried the Tigers on his back against Syracuse with 27 rushes for 203 yards and three touchdowns. (Ken Ruinard/Anderson Independent Mail)

REMEMBER BRICE'S FOURTH QUARTER: IT MAY DEFINE THE TIGERS SEASON

Backup leads Clemson to victory when Lawrence leaves with injury

By Marcel Louis-Jacques | September 29, 2018

It's not often a non-scoring play's true impact is known immediately upon completion; Clemson fans witnessed one of those moments during Saturday's 27-23 win over Syracuse.

Nearly two hours on the nose after Clemson's worst-case-scenario became a reality, backup quarterback Chase Brice delivered the play of the year with a fourth-down conversion on ultimately the Tigers' game-winning drive.

"Game on the line and he throws a strike," head coach Dabo Swinney said. "Unbelievable moxie of Chase. I'm really proud of him."

Starting quarterback Trevor Lawrence's first career start came to an abrupt end late in the second quarter, when a cringeworthy collision sent him to the locker room for the remainder of the day. Clemson remained within striking distance for most of the second half with Brice under center but largely on the strength of Travis Etienne's career-day — not Brice's arm.

"I told Tony and Jeff in the third quarter, 'boys, we're going to have to do this the old-fashioned way.' And somewhere, Danny Ford and Gene Stallings are probably drinking a beer and celebrating," Swinney said. "That was an old-school, old-school way of winning a game. That's what we had to do because we needed to kind of settle Chase down.

"If we couldn't support him with the run game, we probably would've been in trouble."

People generally fear what they don't know or understand, and with eight career pass attempts entering Saturday's game, Clemson fans did not know Chase Brice and feared what could happen if Lawrence was forced out of the game. Swinney insisted, however, that Clemson could win with the redshirt freshman.

The defining drive of Brice's collegiate career began on Clemson's six-yard line with six minutes remaining in the game. His team trailing by three, Brice had 94 yards to his place in Clemson lore; his teammates would make sure he got there.

"When I went in, everybody just kind of rallied around me. It's amazing what you can do when you have teammates who believe in you," Brice said. "I tried to believe in myself, that I could lead the team down (the field), score some points and win. Really they just rallied around me and kept encouraging me."

Clemson's first six plays of the drive — all runs — gained 45 yards; the seventh set it up with a 4th-and-1 from Syracuse's 49-yard line.

When the time came to decide whether to go for it or punt and hope for a stop, Swinney said he made the obvious choice.

"No way was I giving the ball back to (Syracuse quarterback Eric Dungey) in that situation," he said. "We were either going to win it or lose it right there. We still had a couple timeouts, but I'm not going to volunteer to give him the ball."

Chase Brice lines up at quarterback during the fourth quarter of Clemson's come-from-behind win over Syracuse. (Ken Ruinard/Anderson Independent Mail)

Clemson converted with an inside handoff to Etienne — only to have the play blown dead. False start on offensive lineman Gage Cervenka.

It didn't shake Brice's confidence. He picked up his teammate the same way he'd been picked up throughout the game and moved on, promptly earning the first down on a 20-yard strike to Tee Higgins.

"I just told Gage, 'it's OK, we'll get it right here no matter what,'" Brice said. "They created a perfect pocket for me, all I had to do was deliver a ball to Tee."

"We went with a two-safety type of call, a little corner by Tee and a flat route by the tight end to try to hold the corner down," Swinney said. "If I remember correctly, the corner kind of drifted just a little bit, so we kind of had a little window between the guy over the top and the guy underneath.

"Tee did a nice job of breaking his route off underneath over-the-top coverage, and Chase threw a strike. He just threw a strike."

Brice wasn't done; he followed the first down to Higgins with a 17-yard run on the quarterback keeper and Etienne punched in the game-winning touchdown four plays later.

Eight weeks ago, Brice was Clemson's third-string quarterback when the team opened fall camp. Eight months ago, he looked like the odd man out in a loaded quarterback room. But on Saturday, he was "the guy" when his number was called, creating a moment — and a drive — neither he, nor Clemson will ever forget.

"Chase proved he can go in there and be a heck of a player for us," Swinney said. "In the long run, this will be a defining moment for this football team. I'm glad we didn't lose the game, but it'll be a defining moment because of how they responded, how they came together. It was incredible.

"He will never forget this."

If Clemson makes the College Football Playoff, fans may remember the regular season for the team's stout defense or perhaps a memorable performance or two from Lawrence.

Whichever memory you choose to cherish, be sure to give Brice's fourth quarter its due consideration. ■

Chase Brice rushes for 17 yards for a first down against the Orange. Brice, Clemson's third-string quarterback entering the season, also completed 7 of 13 pass attempts in leading Clemson to a 27-23 comeback win. (Ken Ruinard/Anderson Independent Mail)

Clemson 63, Wake Forest 3
October 6, 2018 | Winston-Salem, North Carolina

BIG PLAY DAY

Tigers score 6 touchdowns of at least 55 yards in record-setting win
By Scott Keepfer

Wake Forest coach Dave Clawson fired defensive coordinator Jay Sawvel two weeks ago.

Sawvel was probably counting his blessings late Saturday afternoon.

Travis Etienne rushed for 167 yards on only 10 carries and the Tigers scored six touchdowns of 55 yards or more en route to a 63-3 victory against the Demon Deacons.

It marked the largest margin of victory ever for Clemson in an Atlantic Coast Conference game.

"I didn't see this coming," Clawson said.

Kind of like a freight train emerging from a tunnel.

The Dixie Classic Fair was under way nearby, but Clemson effectively turned Wake Forest's BB&T Stadium into a carnival of its own.

Clemson amassed 698 total yards, including 471 rushing — the fourth-highest total in school history and the most ever under coach Dabo Swinney. The Tigers' average of 11.8 yards per carry set a program standard.

The Tigers had three running backs with more than 100 yards for the first time since 2006. Freshman Lyn-J Dixon added 163 yards on 10 carries, and Adam Choice had 128 yards on 10 attempts.

"It was a baptism by fire," Clawson said. "We've got to own it. Clemson played great. We played poorly. We got embarrassed."

Clemson had developed a big-play reputation long before Saturday, but the Tigers' latest in its streak of 10 consecutive victories against Wake Forest took it to another level.

"That's what every team dreams of being able to do," Swinney said. "That's the one thing that's been consistent in six games — we've been really, really explosive. We've been inefficient at times, and then 'Bam!' we'll get an explosive play. Last year we were efficient, but we weren't very explosive."

The Tigers' six plays of 50 yards or more, each of which resulted in a touchdown, doubled their season total entering the game. Etienne had scoring runs of 59 and 70 yards. Choice had a 64-yard touchdown run — the longest of his career — and Dixon scored on bursts of 65 and 52 yards.

Then there was quarterback Trevor Lawrence, who returned to the starting role after missing the second half of last week's game against Syracuse because of a neck strain. Playing on his 19th birthday, Lawrence was an efficient 20-of-25 for 175 yards, including touchdown tosses of 55 yards to Justyn Ross and 20 yards to Tee Higgins.

Tigers wide receiver Diondre Overton brings in a 2-yard pass from Chase Brice to score a touchdown in the fourth quarter. Six different Clemson players scored touchdowns in the win over Wake Forest. (Bart Boatwright/The Greenville News)

Ross has four touchdown receptions; three have been 50 yards or longer.

"This is a game we can all gain confidence from," Swinney said. "We complemented each other well."

Big plays have become Clemson's calling card, and the promise of more to come appears evident. Now an open date awaits the Tigers, who given their performance against the Deacons probably wish they could continue playing every Saturday without a break.

"This was great momentum for us going into an open date," Swinney said. "I have a lot of confidence in our team. We're not a finished product by any stretch of the imagination, but we're a team that's getting better."

Dave Clawson might agree. ■

Opposite: Wide receiver Justyn Ross races toward the end zone to score a 55-yard touchdown in the second quarter. Above: Dabo Swinney celebrates with Tigers fans after Clemson's 10th consecutive win over Wake Forest. (Bart Boatwright/The Greenville News)

Clemson 41, N.C. State 7
October 20, 2018 | Clemson, South Carolina

CLEMSON REIGNS SUPREME IN BATTLE OF UNBEATENS

Lawrence shines as Tigers dominate Wolfpack in ACC Atlantic showdown
By Scott Keepfer

By game's end it became clear that N.C. State's defense didn't put Trevor Lawrence "on his back" nearly enough.

Lawrence passed for a career-high 308 yards while also setting career bests for completions (26) and attempts (39) as No. 3 Clemson cruised past No. 15 N.C. State 41-7 Saturday in what was supposed to be a showdown between unbeaten teams for ACC Atlantic Division supremacy.

It really wasn't much of a showdown. Only one team lived up to the billing in front of a season-best crowd of 81,295 at Memorial Stadium.

Lawrence shined brighter than anyone on the field — with the possible exception of wide receiver Tee Higgins, who had a career-best eight receptions, including a 46-yard touchdown.

When Lawrence departed early in the fourth quarter, he'd outdueled N.C. State quarterback Ryan Finley and the Tigers had moved ever closer to a fourth consecutive ACC Atlantic Division title.

The Wolfpack defense managed to sack Lawrence on only two occasions, which meant he spent most of the afternoon upright and methodically dissecting a Wolfpack secondary that had received precious little testing in its 5-0 start.

N.C. State stacked the box to stop Clemson's vaunted run game, essentially daring Lawrence to pass. He proved more than willing to accommodate.

"I felt real comfortable today," Lawrence said. "Most of our plays we can check out of and do a lot of different stuff to make it hard on the defense."

Lawrence showed precision and snap on almost all of his throws, which bodes well as the Tigers head down the home stretch with the 19-year-old quarterback firmly in control of this team's fate.

Finley, the Wolfpack's veteran quarterback and the ACC's leading passer, was supposed to be the star of the show, not the long-haired freshman from small-town Georgia. But it was Lawrence who showed coolness and savvy while Finley struggled to provide the Wolfpack offense with any semblance of consistency.

Clemson's defense had plenty of input in that regard, of course, but more was expected out of a quarterback and receiving corps that entered the game with impressive credentials.

Instead it was Lawrence who made the plays, looked cool under pressure and took another big step in just his third start.

"It's a good feeling knowing that we played well but can play a lot better," Lawrence said.

Running back Lyn-J Dixon scores Clemson's final touchdown of the day against N.C. State, giving the Tigers a 41-7 lead. (Ken Ruinard/Anderson Independent Mail)

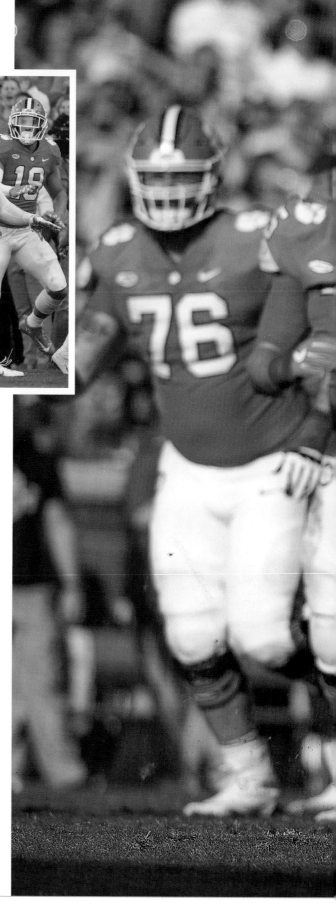

Some other takeaways from the Tigers' seventh consecutive victory against the Wolfpack:

Not that it really mattered, but Clemson's running game, which entered ranked fourth in the nation with a 281-yard average, was held to a season-low 91 yards and Travis Etienne's streak of four games with at least 100 yards came to a crashing halt.

Etienne, who was held to a season-low 39 yards, came through in another way, however, scoring three touchdowns, all of which came from close range — 3, 2 and 1 yards. His three rushing touchdowns made him the first player in Clemson history to rush for three touchdowns in three consecutive games.

"Travis has been awesome," co-offensive coordinator Jeff Scott said. "And three games in a row with three touchdowns is pretty special."

Clemson's secondary was impressive and continued to show growth since its near-debacle at Texas A&M

Above: K'Von Wallace returns in interception 49 yards in the second quarter. (Ken Ruinard/Anderson Independent Mail)
Opposite: Quarterback Trevor Lawrence carries the ball against the Wolfpack. Lawrence completed 26 of 39 passes for 308 yards in the win. (Bart Boatwright/The Greenville News)

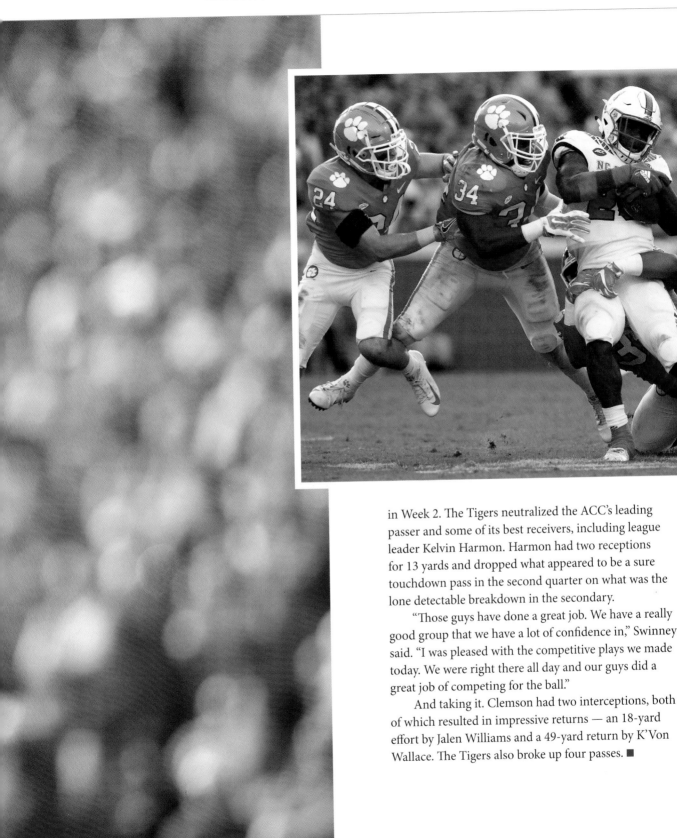

in Week 2. The Tigers neutralized the ACC's leading passer and some of its best receivers, including league leader Kelvin Harmon. Harmon had two receptions for 13 yards and dropped what appeared to be a sure touchdown pass in the second quarter on what was the lone detectable breakdown in the secondary.

"Those guys have done a great job. We have a really good group that we have a lot of confidence in," Swinney said. "I was pleased with the competitive plays we made today. We were right there all day and our guys did a great job of competing for the ball."

And taking it. Clemson had two interceptions, both of which resulted in impressive returns — an 18-yard effort by Jalen Williams and a 49-yard return by K'Von Wallace. The Tigers also broke up four passes. ■

Opposite: Tee Higgins' 46-yard touchdown catch gave Clemson a 14-0 lead in the first quarter. Above: Clemson's defense limited previously undefeated N.C. State to just 297 yards total offense. (Bart Boatwright/The Greenville News)

PIECES IN PLACE FOR COLLEGE FOOTBALL PLAYOFF RUN

Secondary steps up, shuts down N.C. State QB Finley

By Manie Robinson | October 20, 2018

More than 81,000 fans filled Clemson Memorial Stadium on Saturday afternoon. Someone else finally decided to show up too.

Fall.

A cool wind snapped through the air. For most of the morning, the sun hid behind the clouds and painted the sky a solemn gray. It peaked out right before kickoff. It was a welcome alternative to the unseasonably sweltering October heat that previously blanketed the stands.

For the first time this year, everything around Death Valley finally felt like football season. And for the first time this year, it felt like the Clemson team everyone anticipated was finally on that field.

Clemson compiled a dominant performance in every facet of the game. The Tigers dismantled rival North Carolina State, earned a 41-7 victory and dismissed any doubts about their position in the Top 4.

Clemson flashed its potential in sections through the previous six games. Freshman quarterback Trevor Lawrence transitioned seamlessly into the starting role. The receiving corps appeared deeper than the Mariana Trench. The only thing deeper was the defensive line.

Sophomore running back Travis Etienne steered the rushing attack directly toward the top of the record book. The linebackers were reliable. The specialists were solid.

None of that changed Saturday. Yet, one piece of Clemson's College Football Playoff puzzle was missing. That piece was emphatically shoved into place.

The secondary was not tested often during the first half of the semester. Clemson faced three teams that specialize in the run-heavy, triple-option offense. Furman, Georgia Southern and Georgia Tech combined for 26 pass attempts against Clemson.

The Tigers defended 40 attempts against Texas A&M. But not well.

Clemson surrendered 430 yards to the Aggies, merely 57 yards fewer than it allowed in its other five games combined. The secondary softened the sting of that performance with a game-saving interception on Texas A&M's desperate final two-point attempt, but the blatant blemishes cast a cloud of uncertainty.

Syracuse and Wake Forest were not equipped to offer an adequate test. North Carolina State presented the secondary with a make-up exam. Clemson aced it.

N.C. State quarterback Ryan Finley passed for 1,621 yards, 10 touchdowns and three interceptions through his first five games. He completed 69.5 percent of his attempts.

However, Clemson revealed on Finley's first throw that the passes he completed easily against Georgia State and James Madison would not be permitted in Death Valley.

Finley released an accurate pass on an out route to the right side. N.C. State receiver Kelvin Harmon appeared open, but Clemson corner A.J. Terrell closed the opening quickly. Terrell swatted the ball away and set a tone of defiance that Clemson sustained for the entire contest.

Finley did not surpass 100 yards until the third quarter. By then, his completion percentage had dipped below 60 percent. He averaged 4.6 yards per attempt, four yards fewer than he averaged through the previous five games.

Safety Tanner Muse notched his first career sack off Finley on a clean blitz. Nickel back Isaiah Simmons

Defensive back Tanner Muse sacks N.C. State quarterback Ryan Finley during the first quarter. Finley was sacked twice and threw two interceptions in one of the Tigers' strongest defensive efforts of the season. (Bart Boatwright/The Greenville News)

nearly notched another in the second half on a similar play. He did smash into Finley soon enough to disrupt a third-down pass.

Safety K'Von Wallace grabbed an interception off a tipped pass in the second half and carved through the Wolfpack for a masterful 46-yard return.

Clemson closed the game with 10 tackles for loss and four pass breakups. The Tigers allowed 297 yards total offense. Clemson has limited five of its first seven opponents to fewer than 300 yards.

"N.C. State's a good football team. They just ran into a team today that played to its potential," Clemson coach Dabo Swinney said. "We're in a good place. We're improving. No way is our best football behind us. The biggest thing is these guys are eager to improve. They know what they want, and they're willing to put the work in to achieve that."

The secondary answered the question that followed it from Texas. Now, the only question is if Clemson can maintain this level of execution through the remainder of its schedule. The Tigers will not face another Top 25 team. They will not face a quarterback as talented as Finley.

But, regardless of how weak it may appear on paper, each subsequent opponent provides Clemson an opportunity to sharpen and polish, in preparation for a loftier aim.

Clemson proved Saturday that neither its level of play nor its national prominence is contingent on its ACC colleagues. Clemson must perform beyond the strength of its schedule, beyond the caliber of its conference.

Clemson's gauge is not in Tallahassee, Raleigh, Chapel Hill or Charlottesville. It is in Tuscaloosa, Columbus, Baton Rouge and South Bend.

Clemson cannot look past Florida State or Duke or South Carolina, but it can look through them. It can use these next five tests to secure Advanced Placement in the College Football Playoff.

Clemson's Playoff runs are turning into an annual event. For Clemson fans, fall would not feel quite the same without one. ■

Clemson 59, Florida State 10
October 27, 2018 | Tallahassee, Florida

A LAUGHER

Tigers demolish Seminoles in FSU's worst-ever loss at Doak Campbell Stadium
By Manie Robinson

For nearly two decades, Florida State was the bright banner the Atlantic Coast Conference proudly waved. It brightened outlooks with majestic flamboyance. The banner signified the grand laurels an ACC program could achieve.

On Saturday, that banner flapped like a tattered cloth, and Clemson blew through it briskly.

Clemson demolished the Seminoles 59-10. It is the worst loss Florida State has suffered in the history of Doak Campbell Stadium.

Clemson's dominance was laudable. It quickly became laughable. The Tigers were so comfortable in their operation they telegraphed touchdowns for tight end Garrett Williams and defensive tackle Christian Wilkins.

Wilkins' lone carry was a 1-yard plunge across the goal line. He finished with more rushing yards than Florida State, which netted a loss of 21.

"I thought, when I signed up to Florida State, I would never lose like this in my life," FSU defensive tackle Marvin Wilson said.

No one else expected this outcome, either, considering the recent history of this rivalry. This game used to draw national attention. It ultimately decided the conference champion. It propelled the victor into the national title race.

On Saturday, it was an exhibition of Clemson's extravagant talent. And another embarrassing exposition in the rapid dilapidation of a former powerhouse.

Clemson has held the ACC crown for three consecutive years, but even in those victorious campaigns, Florida State was a formidable foe, a respectable contender. This year, the Seminoles could miss a bowl for the first time in 37 seasons.

"I've been on the other end of these butt-whoopings, too" said Clemson coach Dabo Swinney, who referenced the 51-14 loss the Tigers suffered against Florida State in 2013. "This is one of those moments where you probably just burn the tape and go on to the next one."

This was not the first blowout of the season for Clemson. It most likely will not be the last. Clemson swept through Furman, Georgia Southern, Wake Forest and North Carolina State by a combined score of 190-24.

In those blowouts, there was a distinct discrepancy in talent and depth. But there was no perceptible gap in effort. Those teams were overmatched. They were not overwhelmed.

Conversely, the Seminoles' roster is filled with championship-level talent, but their lack of execution and organization was glaring. Their sporadic lack of effort was alarming.

Defensive lineman Xavier Thomas brings down Florida State running back Anthony Grant during the first quarter of Clemson's 59-10 win. Florida state netted -21 rushing yards on the day. (Bart Boatwright/The Greenville News)

The Florida State pregame ritual was foreboding. The Seminole mascot, Osceola, normally rides a horse to midfield and plants a spear aggressively into the turf. On Saturday, Osceola hurled the spear toward the ground, but it fell flat.

That is precisely how Florida State performed. The Seminoles lay flat as Clemson stepped over them.

"First time since I've been here I felt like we had some guys that quit on our football team," first-year FSU coach Willie Taggart said. "That can't be tolerated. One thing you can't do, you can't quit."

Earlier in the week, Swinney praised the talent on Florida State's roster. He commended the Seminoles' championship heritage. He acknowledged the daunting atmosphere in Tallahassee.

Opposite: Defensive lineman Christian Wilkins lined up in the backfield and scored a touchdown on a 1-yard run in the second quarter. Above: Linebacker Tre Lamar returns an interception 43 yards into Seminole territory. (Bart Boatwright/The Greenville News)

However, the talent Swinney referenced produced no threat. The program he revered is a fading memory. The atmosphere he anticipated was replaced with empty seats.

Swinney politely asserted confidence that Florida State would not rest in this valley much longer.

"Willie will get it going here," Swinney said. "This is a tough time for them from a transition standpoint. Not only are they all new coaches, but they're trying to do things in a different way. It takes a little time."

Not many others who watched the game share Swinney's optimism. Doak Campbell was a sobering scene, a cautionary revelation of how swiftly a program can descend from its perch of power.

On the field, the Tigers showed no sympathy for Florida State's fall. It is not Clemson's responsibility to extend its arm over the cliff and pull its rival back up.

Clemson's only obligation is to its objective — another ACC championship and another shot at the College Football Playoff. Not even the substandard status of the ACC can impede that.

Clemson is enrolled in an elite class. Its grade is not contingent on the rest of the league. Florida State was once a star student in that class. This season, the Seminoles dropped out.

The ACC has lowered that tattered Florida State banner. In its place, the league has raised an orange and white flag. Clemson now holds the swagger and the splendor. Swinney has developed a culture of consistency, diligence and excellence that can ensure Clemson's banner will withstand any maelstrom and continue to fly high. ■

Defensive back A.J. Terrell tackles Florida State running back Cam Akers (3) during the first quarter. Clemson's 59-10 win was Florida State's worst loss in the history of Doak Campbell Stadium. (Bart Boatwright/The Greenville News)

Clemson 77, Louisville 16
November 3, 2018 | Clemson, South Carolina

EVERYBODY IN

88 Tigers take the field, 9 score in rout of Cardinals
By Scott Keepfer

If, as Clemson coach Dabo Swinney says, the fun indeed is in the winning, his players must be having the time of their lives.

The latest installment of the Tigers' Fall Frolic 2018 came Saturday at Memorial Stadium, where a 77-16 bludgeoning of Louisville unfolded in front of 78,741 fans.

The primary conclusion: One knows things are going well when Trevor Lawrence passes for 59 yards and the Tigers win by 61 points.

No. 2-ranked Clemson has made a mockery of the competition of late, winning its past four games by a combined 240-36 and relishing the opportunity to play as many people in a game as care to don an orange jersey.

The Tigers will enter next week's trip to Boston College 9-0, including 6-0 in Atlantic Coast Conference play, and intent on wrapping up a fourth consecutive league title and a lofty spot in the College Football Playoff.

To Clemson's credit, the team isn't just going through the motions against outclassed competition. In fact, the second- and third-team players appear to be attempting to upstage the guys ahead of them at every chance.

Nine players scored touchdowns on Saturday, and one of them wears No. 90 and checks in at 6-foot-4, 350 pounds. Dexter Lawrence took his turn in the Tigers' jumbo package, and the result was a 2-yard touchdown run, matching the score turned in by his svelte backfield mate — 315-pound Christian Wilkins — last week at Florida State.

"Coach Swinney told me that it was my time to shine," Lawrence said.

Former Alabama coach Gene Stallings, who coached Swinney with the Crimson Tide in the early 1990s, was in the crowd Saturday, so maybe the play call was as much for him as it was for Lawrence, who said it was his first touchdown "probably since middle school."

"I know he (Stallings) was smiling when we lined up in the I formation and handed it to big No. 90," Swinney said.

A second conclusion: When you're alternating defensive tackles in the offensive backfield, things are going well.

At the outset of Saturday's game, Clemson made its 400th trek down "The Hill" at Death Valley since the tradition began in 1942.

That's when things began to go downhill for Louisville.

Clemson scored two touchdowns in its first five plays, setting the tone for the punishment that ensued. By the time the proceedings came to a merciful end late in the afternoon, the Tigers had amassed 661 yards total offense, including a season-high 492 rushing — the fifth-best total in program history.

Clemson averaged a gaudy 13.3 yards per rush and

Will Swinney gets a hug from his father, Clemson coach Dabo Swinney, following Will Swinney's first career touchdown catch in the fourth quarter. (Bart Boatwright/The Greenville News)

a school-record 11.6 yards per play in the rout. So many Clemson players got in on the fun — 88, to be exact — that the most tired Tiger at game's end was the mascot, who had to endure a physically exhausting afternoon that included 462 celebratory push-ups.

On the field, Clemson spread the wealth much like Swinney has done all season. The benefits are becoming more evident as the season winds down.

"It's not a selfish group," Clemson co-offensive coordinator Jeff Scott said. "You've got to be selfless to play offense at Clemson, because we've got a lot of guys and you're not always going to get the opportunities."

As in the Wake Forest game a few weeks before, Clemson had three running backs with more than 100 yards rushing, led by sophomore Travis Etienne, who maximized his touches by darting for 153 yards on eight carries and pushing himself to within two yards of the first 1,000-yard campaign of his young career.

Not be outdone, Tavien Feaster rushed for 101 yards, including a 70-yard touchdown, and freshman Lyn-J Dixon completed the package with a 116-yard day.

"I remember a day when we were just trying to get one running back over 100 yards," Scott said.

Other notable moments included back-up quarterback Chase Brice coming in and completing six of seven passes — half of which went for touchdowns, and Swinney's eldest son, Will, putting his holding duties on hold long enough to score the first touchdown of his career on an 8-yard pass from Brice with 8:52 remaining.

It also was a good day for left tackle Mitch Hyatt, a three-time All-ACC selection who set a Clemson standard for career snaps on Saturday, then talked about getting better.

"We didn't score on every drive," Hyatt said. "So there's always something to improve on."

Don't tell Louisville coach Bobby Petrino that.

"We couldn't stop them," Petrino said.

It sure seemed that way, regardless of vantage point.

It was the highest-scoring game for Clemson since an 82-24 victory against Wake Forest during its 1981 national championship season and extended Louisville's losing streak to six games, dropping the Cardinals to 2-7, including 0-6 in the ACC. ■

Freshman receiver Justyn Ross catches a touchdown pass from Chase Brice in the third quarter. Ross was Clemson's leading receiver with two catches for 74 yards. (Bart Boatwright/The Greenville News)

Clemson 27, Boston College 7
November 10, 2018 | Chestnut Hill, Massachusetts

DIVISION CHAMPS!

Defense steals the spotlight as Tigers win fourth straight ACC Atlantic title

By Scott Keepfer

The videotape from this one likely won't reside in Dabo Swinney's collection of personal favorites, but the result had him smiling late Saturday night and Trevor Lawrence wearing a leather helmet circa 1940.

Clemson struggled for much of the game but pulled away late to post a 27-7 victory against Boston College that gave the Tigers their fourth consecutive Atlantic Coast Conference Atlantic Division title and the opportunity for a fourth straight ACC Championship.

Clemson (10-0, including 7-0 in ACC games) will play the ACC's Coastal Division winner at Bank of America Stadium in Charlotte on Dec. 1.

The victory was Clemson's eighth in a row against the Eagles (7-3, 4-2) and clinched an eighth consecutive season with 10 or more victories, extending a program record.

Clemson's offensive effort was disjointed at best, but the Tigers came up with big plays when it had to have them. Lawrence, the Tigers' freshman quarterback, completed 29 of 40 passes for 295 yards with a touchdown and was recipient of the game's Most Valuable Player award, which in this case is a replica leather helmet like the one worn by Clemson great Banks McFadden in the 1940 Cotton Bowl against Boston College.

"It's really cool," Lawrence said. "It was cool for us to play well in a big game."

While Lawrence sported the leather helmet, it was Amari Rodgers who sealed the deal, weaving 58 yards for a punt return touchdown that essentially put a bow on the victory with 11:39 left in the game.

"That was great to see — especially to bounce back from the tough play earlier on the other punt return," co-offensive coordinator Jeff Scott said.

Rodgers fumbled a punt earlier in the game, but Swinney stuck with the sophomore.

"It's something we talk about all the time — 'hey, bad things are going to happen, how are you going to respond?'" Scott said. "Great players go back and make up for it. He wanted to go back and get one."

But Clemson's defense was the star of the game, particularly after Boston College quarterback Anthony Brown was injured and left the game for good on the Eagles' sixth play from scrimmage after absorbing a hit from Clemson defensive tackle Christian Wilkins.

The Tigers held Boston College to a season-low 113 total yards and running back AJ Dillon — the ACC's leading rusher — to a season-low 39 yards on 16 carries.

"It was a good night," said safety Tanner Muse, who

Clemson players douse head coach Dabo Swinney with Gatorade following Clemson's 27-7 win over Boston College to clinch the ACC Atlantic Division title. (Bart Boatwright/The Greenville News)

led the team with 10 tackles. "All in all, we did a pretty good job. We take a lot of pride in this because they run the ball and score a lot of points."

Until Saturday night. Clemson not only kept Dillon in check but allowed only 0.3 yards per rush while accumulating 10 tackles for loss.

Despite that, Clemson held only a 13-7 halftime lead after outgaining Boston College 240-23.

The Tigers looked as if they might be jump-starting their fourth consecutive blowout victory when they opened the game with a seven-play, 59-yard scoring drive highlighted by a 41-yard completion from Lawrence to Rodgers and ending in Greg Huegel's 30-yard field goal.

After Boston College got a 74-yard punt return for a touchdown by Michael Walker with 6:22 left in the first quarter to give the Eagles their only lead, Clemson promptly marched 70 yards in nine plays to regain the lead. The Tigers lined up in their jumbo package with defensive linemen Dexter Lawrence and Christian Wilkins in the backfield, but Clemson crossed the Eagles up when Lawrence tossed a 2-yard touchdown pass over the defense and into the arms of tight end Milan Richard.

Clemson added a 23-yard field goal by Huegel on its next possession, extending the lead to 13-7.

Lawrence capped a rapid-fire three-play drive with a 6-yard touchdown run on a bootleg to open the second half and give the Tigers some breathing room at 20-7.

"I'm really proud of Trevor," Swinney said. "He's a true freshman, and to come up here in this environment and really lead us ... he's continuing to learn and grow and get better every week."

The Tigers have outscored Boston College 117-23 during the past three meetings. ∎

Wide receiver Amari Rodgers makes a catch during the first quarter. Rodgers had five catches for 73 yards against Boston College. (Bart Boatwright/The Greenville News)

Clemson 35, Duke 6
November 17, 2018 | Clemson, South Carolina

CLEMSON SHRUGS OFF SLOW START

Tigers score 35 straight points, improve record to 11-0
By Scott Keepfer

Clemson's preferred operating procedure is to strike early and often and then turn the game over to its defense.

The Tigers took a different approach Saturday night against Duke.

After a lethargic start during which the visiting Blue Devils took a 6-0 lead into the second quarter, Clemson's offense — led by running back Travis Etienne — picked up the pace, scoring 35 consecutive points to remain undefeated and on track for a fourth consecutive College Football Playoff berth.

"I'm really disappointed in how we started, but the good news is it's a four-quarter game," Clemson coach Dabo Swinney said. "The guys came out and dominated the second half in all phases."

Etienne appeared frustrated in the early going and had only four yards on five carries in the first half. But the sophomore rushed for 77 yards on four carries in the second half, including touchdown runs of 27 and 29 yards, to key the Tigers' late scoring barrage.

His two scores gave him 17 rushing touchdowns this season, trying Travis Zachery for the school's season record.

But it wasn't all Etienne. Freshman quarterback Trevor Lawrence had a solid game despite a lot of dropped passes, completing 21 of 38 attempts for 251 yards with a pair of scores — 19 yards to Justyn Ross and 10 yards to T.J. Chase.

"We dropped more balls tonight than any game all year," Swinney said. "If we don't drop those balls, we would have had over 500 yards (of offense)."

The primary immediate concern as the Tigers turn their focus to the annual Palmetto Bowl against rival South Carolina as well as the postseason is the health of graduate wide receiver Hunter Renfrow. Renfrow was injured while attempting to make a reception with 9:36 left in the second quarter and did not return.

"He's being evaluated," Swinney said. "He was good in the locker room, but we'll know more tomorrow."

Clemson's third-leading receiver with 36 catches this season, Renfrow earlier caught a pass in a 39th consecutive game, breaking the school record held by Artavis Scott.

Clemson improved to 11-0 for the fourth time in school history and the second time in the past four years. The Tigers also finished 8-0 in the Atlantic Coast Conference, marking the seventh time the Tigers have gone unbeaten in league play.

The victory was the 51st in four years for Clemson's seniors, setting a program and ACC record. Clemson

Clemson wide receiver T.J. Chase hauls in a 10-yard pass from Trevor Lawrence for a touchdown in the fourth quarter. (Bart Boatwright/The Greenville News)

is only the second school to produce a 51-win class, joining Alabama, which has produced classes of 53 wins (2014-17) and 51 wins (2013-16 and 2015-18).

Clemson, which wrapped up its fourth consecutive ACC Atlantic Division title last week, will play Pittsburgh (7-4, 6-1) in the ACC Championship Game on Dec. 1 at Bank of America Stadium in Charlotte, N.C.

Duke, which will go bowling for the fifth time in six years, slipped to 7-4, 3-4.

Duke, which was playing Clemson for the first time since 2012, gave the Tigers all they could handle early, outgaining Clemson 127-37 in the first quarter and taking a 6-0 lead.

But Clemson took command in the second quarter, getting a 2-yard run from Tavien Feaster to cap a seven-play, 75-yard drive early and then a 19-yard touchdown pass from Lawrence to freshman wide receiver Justyn Ross just before the half for a 14-6 lead at the break.

The running game came out recharged in the second half. Etienne averaged more than 19 yards per carry in the second half, and the Tigers finished with 208 yards rushing.

Clemson's defense also picked things up in the second half and kept steady pressure on Duke quarterback Daniel Jones. Jones, who passed for 361 yards and rushed for 186 more in a win against North Carolina the week before, had 158 yards passing and seven yards rushing on 12 carries.

He was under constant duress and was sacked four times by the Tigers, who amassed nine tackles for loss and held the Blue Devils to a season-low 262 total yards.

"At the end of the day, they've been playing football at Clemson for a long, long time, and this is only the fourth team to be 11-0," Swinney said. "What a great accomplishment for our guys. They have been unbelievable leaders and I'm really proud of how they've developed. It was a great night overall, and we're excited to be where we are." ■

Derion Kendrick leaps over a Duke defender as he returns the opening kickoff 19 yards. (Bart Boatwright/The Greenville News)

FEARSOME FOURSOME

Defensive line is leaving its mark on program — and opposing quarterbacks

Manie Robinson | November 17, 2018

Duke has sharp uniforms. They are simple. The two shoulder stripes flow cleanly through the two stripes down the pants leg. The simplistic two-tone ensemble would look good on any field or any runway.

However, by the fourth quarter Saturday night, Duke quarterback Daniel Jones had the ugliest uniform in the stadium. It was filthy, sullied by repeated falls on that cold, worn field in Death Valley.

Jones could wear it as a badge of honor. He exhibited his toughness as he absorbed every hit. He was chased down. Blindsided. Folded. Scattered. Smothered. And covered.

Clemson sacked Jones four times through the first three quarters during its 35-6 victory. Defensive end Clelin Ferrell notched two of those sacks. He is technically a junior, but Ferrell was honored during the pregame Senior Day ceremonies. All-American tackle Christian Wilkins and defensive end Austin Bryant were celebrated as well.

Along with junior tackle Dexter Lawrence, Clemson's starting defensive line has garnered national attention for its dominance and its personality. The linemen outmaneuver blockers with their rush moves and celebrate their tackles with dance moves.

Every game is decided in the trenches. Where heads knock on each snap. Where momentum is harnessed or exchanged. It is no coincidence that Clemson has won 51 games during the four seasons Wilkins has led the defensive line.

On Saturday, Clemson's defensive front disrupted one of the most polished passers and dangerous scramblers in the Atlantic Coast Conference. Ferrell, Wilkins, Bryant and Lawrence turned Duke's backfield into a backyard. They played a physical game of tag and chased Jones out of the pocket.

Jones averaged 243.5 passing yards through the previous 10 games. He threw for 158 yards Saturday. Jones rushed for 186 yards the previous week against North Carolina. He netted seven yards against Clemson.

Clemson is guaranteed merely three more games with its fearsome and fun foursome. At some point, every Clemson fan, hater and objective observer must step back and sincerely ponder what we have been watching.

Great players come along every recruiting cycle. Great groups cycle through less frequently.

Clemson will reload its roster. Freshman Xavier Thomas is already equipped to succeed and even exceed Ferrell on the edge. The parts will be replaced, but Clemson could never replace the whole.

This defensive line group is the equivalent of the DeAndre Hopkins-Sammy Watkins-Martavis Bryant receiving corps Clemson enjoyed in 2011 and 2012. Those of us fortunate enough to witness that

Clemson defensive linemen Christian Wilkins (42) and Clelin Ferrell (99) celebrate after sacking Boston College quarterback Anthony Brown. (Bart Boatwright/The Greenville News)

combination accepted its excellence as a standard. The further we move away from that tenure, the more that trio excelled in the National Football League, the more we can appreciate its greatness.

These four linemen have graced Sports Illustrated covers and sat for national television interviews. They are larger-than-life characters. But through the next three games, do not allow their exposure to overshadow their excellence.

Do not allow the focus on wins and losses, rankings and standings to sap the sheer delight from the game. Do not allow the dances and pranks to diminish their dominance.

Forget the sacks and post-sack choreography. Pay more attention to the physical and technical marvels these linemen are. Watch Ferrell's hands and angles. Study Wilkins' first step. Examine Lawrence's power and balance. Observe Bryant's strength and leverage.

Even under the glow of the limelight, this foursome can easily be taken for granted. Appreciate the substance. Savor the performance. Enjoy the headlines. But notice the fine print.

These professors of the pass rush offer weekly seminars on sacks. Bring a notebook. There are only three courses left on the syllabus. ∎

Clelin Ferrell (99), Dexter Lawrence (90), and Christian Wilkins (42) bring down Duke wide receiver Johnathan Lloyd (5). Clemson's defensive line was also responsible for four sacks during the Tigers' decisive win over the Blue Devils. (Bart Boatwright/The Greenville News)

Clemson 56, South Carolina 35
November 24, 2018 | Clemson, South Carolina

CLEMSON CAPTURES FIFTH CONSECUTIVE STATE CHAMPIONSHIP

Tigers improve to 12-0 for second time in program history

By Scott Keepfer

Clemson's secondary showed plenty of holes that need mending, but the No. 2 Tigers had enough offensive firepower to hold off South Carolina and Jake Bentley on a chilly and foggy Saturday night at Memorial Stadium.

Quarterback Trevor Lawrence passed for a career-high 393 yards with a touchdown and running back Travis Etienne rushed for 150 yards with two touchdowns as Clemson overcame a career-best performance by Bentley to defeat the Gamecocks for the fifth consecutive year.

Clemson improved to 12-0 for the second time in program history and remained on track for a fourth consecutive berth in the College Football Playoff.

"To be 12-0 is really special, and to win five in a row in the state championship is a rare thing," Clemson coach Dabo Swinney said. "It was an amazing performance offensively — one of the best games I've ever been around offensively and we left some on the table."

The Tigers will put their unblemished record and No. 2 ranking on the line Saturday against Pittsburgh in the Atlantic Coast Conference Championship Game in Charlotte, N.C.

Clemson and South Carolina combined for 1,344 yards, falling seven yards short of matching the program record for combined yardage in a game set by Clemson and N.C. State in 2012.

South Carolina's Bentley passed for a career-high 510 yards, the second-highest total ever against Clemson, with five touchdowns.

"That was about as bad of a performance on the back end that we've ever had," Swinney said. "They had a great plan. They spread us out and we had a bunch of busts and uncontested throws."

South Carolina's passing game torched Clemson time and again, but it wasn't enough against a high-scoring Clemson team that amassed 744 total yards — the third-highest total in school history — including 351 yards and seven touchdowns rushing.

Lawrence, a freshman, completed 27 of 36 passes, and his 393 yards were the most ever by a Clemson quarterback in the program's 116 games against South Carolina.

"I thought Trevor was amazing," Swinney said. "In that arena, on that stage, he was awesome."

Etienne's touchdown runs of 2 and 7 yards gave him 19, breaking the school's season record. He has six 100-yard games and pushed his season rushing total to 1,307 yards, which moved him ahead of six players and into

Clemson wide receiver Tee Higgins (5) makes a reception over South Carolina cornerback Rashad Fenton (16). Freshman quarterback Trevor Lawrence completed 27 of 36 passes as Clemson maintained its perfect record. (Bart Boatwright/The Greenville News)

fourth place on the Tigers' season rushing chart.

Adam Choice added three short touchdown runs for the Tigers, Tavien Feaster another and even defensive tackle Christian Wilkins got in on the fun, scoring on a 1-yard run.

Tee Higgins had six receptions for 142 yards and a touchdown and Hunter Renfrow, whose medical status was in doubt and the subject of much speculation after he missed the second half of the Duke game because of an injury last week, played and played well. He had five receptions for 80 yards, extending his school record to 40 consecutive games with at least one catch.

"Renfrow — I mean, 'wow,'" Swinney said. "He's just so much fun to watch."

The Tigers had three drives of 95 yards or more, which also was a first in school history.

Above: Clemson head coach Dabo Swinney celebrates with running back Tavien Feaster (28) after scoring against South Carolina. (Bart Boatwright/The Greenville News) Opposite: Clemson defensive lineman Christian Wilkins (42) soars for a touchdown during the second quarter at Memorial Stadium. (Ken Ruinard/ Anderson Independent Mail)

The teams combined for 709 yards and seven touchdowns in the first half. South Carolina opened by driving 75 yards in 12 plays for a 7-0 lead — the first time Clemson's defense surrendered a first-quarter touchdown this season. Bentley capped the drive with a 9-yard touchdown pass to wide receiver Deebo Samuel.

Clemson responded by scoring 21 consecutive points for a lead it would never relinquish. Choice scored on a 1-yard run, Higgins snagged a 22-yard touchdown pass from Lawrence and Wilkins added his 1-yard touchdown plunge out of the Tigers' "Jumbo package" for a 21-7 lead.

After South Carolina tight end Kiel Pollard scored on a 67-yard pass play from Bentley, Choice scored on a 2-yard run for a 28-14 advantage. But Clemson's defense, which allowed only one touchdown play from scrimmage in excess of 67 yards this season, got burned on back-to-back offensive plays by the Gamecocks as Bentley found Samuel wide open behind the Tigers' secondary for a 75-yard touchdown that pulled South Carolina to 28-21 behind at the half

Clemson scored on each of its first three possessions of the second half to take command. Etienne got the ball rolling with his 2-yard run, Feaster followed with a 13-yard touchdown run and Choice capped off the 21-0 run with a 15-yard run.

Bentley completed 32 of 50 passes, and his 510 yards were the most for a South Carolina quarterback against Clemson. Samuel led all receivers with 10 receptions for 210 yards and three touchdowns while Shi Smith had nine catches for 109 yard and a score. ■

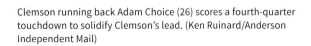

Clemson running back Adam Choice (26) scores a fourth-quarter touchdown to solidify Clemson's lead. (Ken Ruinard/Anderson Independent Mail)

ACC CHAMPIONSHIP GAME

Clemson 42, Pitt 10
December 1, 2018 | Charlotte, North Carolina

PLAYOFF RUSH

Tigers rush for 301 yards in win, seal spot in College Football Playoff
By Scott Keepfer

When faced with a formidable rushing attack, what to do?

Unleash one of your own, apparently.

Clemson's Travis Etienne set the tone by dashing 75 yards for a touchdown on the first play of the game and the Tigers went on to rush for 301 yards — averaging almost nine yards per carry — in a victory against Pitt on a rain-drenched Saturday night in the Atlantic Coast Conference Championship Game at Bank of America Stadium.

It was Clemson's eighth straight win by 20 or more points, a school record, and the seniors' program-record 53rd victory against only four losses the past four years.

"It has been an historic year," Clemson coach Dabo Swinney said. "These guys have done things all year that have never been done or haven't been done in forever, and this was just another one of those things tonight. You can't be the best ever if you don't do things that ain't ever been done."

Etienne finished with 156 yards and two touchdowns as the Tigers claimed their fourth consecutive ACC title and 18th overall — the most in league history.

Etienne, a sophomore running back who this past week was selected ACC Player of the Year, rushed for 100 yards or more for the seventh time this season and pushed his season total to 1,463, the second-highest total

in program history. Wayne Gallman rushed for 1,527 yards in 2015.

"The reason I've been so successful this year is just because of the group of backs that I have," said Etienne, who was selected the game's Most Valuable Player. "Tavien (Feaster) coming in there, just wearing the defense down, Adam (Choice) coming in and you see what he can do, and when Lyn-J (Dixon) gets a chance he's just unbelievable."

The Tigers improved to 13-0 for just the second time in school history and essentially wrapped up a berth in the College Football Playoff for the fourth consecutive year; the Tigers have been ranked No. 2 in each playoff poll this season.

A Dec. 29 matchup against No. 3 Notre Dame in either the Orange Bowl in Miami or the Cotton Bowl in Dallas is expected to be announced on Sunday at noon.

"Aw, shoot, man, just tell us where we're going and we'll be ready to go," Swinney said.

Clemson became the eighth consecutive Atlantic Division team to win the ACC title. Pitt, which won the Coastal Division for the first time since joining the league in 2013, slipped to 7-6, but the Panthers are bowl eligible for the 10th time in 11 years.

The Tigers are 114-30 under Swinney, who this past week was selected ACC Coach of the Year for the second time.

Coach Dabo Swinney holds the Dr. Pepper ACC Championship trophy after the Tigers' 42-10 win over Pittsburgh. (Bart Boatwright/The Greenville News)

The Tigers have won the past two ACC championship games by a combined 80-13, and Saturday night's triumph was sweet redemption for Clemson's seniors, whose lone home loss the past four seasons was a 43-42 to Pitt in the 10th game of the 2016 season.

The outcome was considerably different this time.

Etienne ran 75 yards on the first play for a 7-0 lead. On Pitt's first possession, Clemson linebacker Isaiah Simmons forced a fumble by quarterback Kenny Pickett that was snatched out of the air by defensive tackle Christian Wilkins and returned 18 yards to the Pitt 3-yard line. Etienne scored on the next play for a 14-0 advantage.

Opposite: Part of an essential rushing effort, Clemson running back Lyn-J Dixon (23) scores past Pittsburgh defensive back Dennis Briggs (20) at Bank of America Stadium in Charlotte. Above: Wide receiver Tee Higgins (5) catches a pass in front of Pitt's Jason Pinnock (15) for one of his two touchdowns in the ACC Championship Game. (Bart Boatwright/The Greenville News)

But the Panthers' rushing attack got going midway through the second quarter, resulting in a 62-yard drive capped by a 37-yard field goal from Alex Kessman and a 39-yard drive that Qadree Ollison finished with a 1-yard touchdown run to cut Clemson's lead to 14-10.

It didn't take long for the Tigers to regain control, however, driving 75 yards in seven plays for a 5-yard touchdown pass from quarterback Trevor Lawrence to wide receiver Tee Higgins. Clemson cornerback A.J. Terrell then intercepted a pass by Pickett and returned it 31 yards to the Pitt 10, setting up another Lawrence-to-Higgins score on the next play that provided a 28-10 halftime cushion.

Lawrence has thrown 15 touchdown passes with no interceptions in the red zone this season, but it wasn't his best game overall. The freshman, who was selected ACC Rookie of the Year earlier in the week, completed 12 of 24 passes for 118 yards.

Higgins' second touchdown reception gave him a team-high 10 this season.

Choice added a 1-yard touchdown run on the second play of the final quarter for a 35-10 lead and Dixon wrapped up the evening with a 4-yard scoring run with 3:17 left.

The Tigers' defense, which entered the game ranked second nationally in rushing defense, surrendered a season-high 192 yards, but with little damage. Darrin Hall led the Panthers with 86 yards on 14 carries, pushing his season total to 1,021 yards and, along with Ollison, giving Pitt two 1,000 rushers for the first time.

"When you're playing the No. 2 team in the country, you can't play from behind," Hall said. "You've got to play your best game, and we didn't do that."

Clemson had nine tackles for loss, with defensive tackle Dexter Lawrence and linebacker Tre Lamar wreaking the most havoc with nine and five tackles, respectively. Lawrence had 2.5 tackles for loss while Lamar had two.

The Tigers also became only the second Power 5 team to win four consecutive conference championship games, joining Florida, which accomplished the feat from 1993 to 1996. ■

Clemson players and coaches pose for photos after earning their fourth straight ACC Championship. (Ken Ruinard/Anderson Independent Mail)

9
RUNNING BACK
TRAVIS ETIENNE

Bigger, faster, stronger sophomore emerges as one of the nation's top running backs

By Scott Keepfer | December 26, 2018

Travis Etienne made quite an impression as a freshman. He made an even bigger one this season — literally.

A bigger, stronger, faster Etienne established himself as one of the nation's top running backs while helping Clemson to a 13-0 record and No. 2 national ranking.

Next up? A taste of Notre Dame in the Cotton Bowl.

"I think he's as good a running back as we've seen since Georgia of last year — that kind of talent," Notre Dame coach Brian Kelly said.

Nick Chubb notwithstanding, Etienne may be the best the Fighting Irish have faced in years.

Etienne pinballed his way to 1,463 yards and a school single-season record 21 rushing touchdowns this season, earning first-team All-Atlantic Coast Conference honors as well as league Offensive Player of the Year recognition.

He finished the season with a flourish and will enter the Cotton Bowl on a roll after rushing for 306 yards in the Tigers' last two games, notching his sixth and seventh 100-yard games of the season.

"I worked out in the offseason and put on more weight," said Etienne, who came to campus around 190 pounds and now is shade over 200. "And the coaches just put me in the best position to make plays."

That may indeed be the case, but Etienne does considerable heavy lifting on his own, regardless of the position in which he finds himself. His linemen love blocking for a guy who is so aggressive running the ball.

"He just improves every week," offensive lineman Sean Pollard said. "The offensive linemen want to block for somebody like that.

"It's great. You know if you put that little extra into blocking, he's going to take it to the house. It's nice knowing you've got somebody back there who can break a tackle and go 80 yards like it's nothing."

Given his penchant for breaking runs into the second and third level of the defense, perhaps no one on Clemson's defense knows more about the challenge of tackling Etienne than safety Tanner Muse, who described Etienne as "slippery."

"You never know about him," Muse said. "He'll try

Sophomore running back Travis Etienne celebrates with the Dr. Pepper ACC Championship trophy, his second ACC title as a member of the Clemson team. (Bart Boatwright/The Greenville News)

to run over you sometimes and then try to go around you sometimes.

"I know his freshman year, when he first started coming out, he broke some 60-yard, 50-yard, 40-yard runs just like crazy and you look at our defense from last year and it was a top-tier defense and we kind of took a step back and were like, 'This dude's a freshman?' He's the real deal."

Etienne proved as much this season, backing up his surprising freshman campaign in which he led the Tigers with 766 yards and 13 rushing touchdowns.

"He's really coming into his body," Muse said. "His legs are real thick, tree trunks, and then he's fast. He's got that low center of gravity, so people try to hit him from the side it's not going to work. It's almost like a big Mack truck running down an interstate, you've got to get in front of him, somebody's got to get on the side of him, somebody's got to get on the back of him and somebody's got to get on top of him to get him down.

"He's a big strong dude, but he doesn't look it. People come in and they're 'I'm gonna smoke this dude. He ain't got nothing for me.' And then they figure it out the hard way."

That deceptive power is belied by his uncanny knack for remaining upright.

"I'm a balanced runner," Etienne said.

No kidding.

As he pinballs his way through opposing defenses, he draws oohs and aahs from fans and teammates alike — even those on the sideline.

"We're always peeking at the screen (during games), trying to see what's going on while (defensive coordinator Brent) Venables is trying to make an adjustment or something, and we're like 'How did he get out of that?,'" linebacker Isaiah Simmons said.

"His balance is the key thing. You can't just hit him because his balance is ridiculous; it's amazing. He's so hard to tackle, especially when he gets going, then he's even harder to tackle. He's a really special guy."

After substantial offseason training, Travis Etienne emerged as an undisputed star at running back in 2018. (Josh Morgan/The Greenville News)

Etienne, who is averaging 8.3 yards per carry this season, also acknowledges the importance of having back-ups such as Adam Choice, Tavien Feaster and Lyn-J Dixon — all of whom are averaging 5.8 yards per carry or more.

"We're at our best when we're rotating in and out and keeping everybody with fresh legs," Etienne said.

Etienne finished seventh in Heisman Trophy voting earlier this month, and his teammates believe he was short-changed. But perhaps another record-setting season as a junior will help his cause some next December.

"I think he definitely should've been more of a contender for the Heisman," Pollard said "I mean he splits time. Most of these running backs with all these yards don't split time, so what he does with a limited number of reps is crazy." ■

Opposite: Running back Travis Etienne is interviewed by ESPN during the Cotton Bowl media day at AT&T Stadium in Arlington. (Bart Boatwright/The Greenville News) Above: Etienne stretches during practice for the Cotton Bowl at the Poe Indoor Facility in Clemson. (Ken Ruinard/Anderson Independent Mail)

COTTON BOWL

Clemson 30, Notre Dame 3

December 29, 2018 | Arlington, Texas

FRESHMEN SHINE ON BIG STAGE

Trevor Lawrence, Justyn Ross propel No. 2 Tigers to victory over previously unbeaten Irish

By Scott Keepfer

Once again, the moment wasn't too big for Trevor Lawrence.

Or fellow freshman Justyn Ross, for that matter.

Lawrence and Ross proved a formidable twosome Saturday night in the Cotton Bowl, sparking No. 2 Clemson to a 30-3 domination of previously unbeaten and third-ranked Notre Dame and sending the Tigers to their third College Football Playoff National Championship Game in four years.

No. 2 Clemson improved to 14-0 — tying the school record for wins in a season — and notched its fourth victory in six College Playoff games over the past four years.

"This is what we came here to do," Clemson coach Dabo Swinney said. "This senior group just won their 54th game. Man, we're so excited to have the opportunity to go to California and represent the ACC and play another great opponent."

The Tigers, who are 3-1 all-time against the Fighting Irish, will play No. 1 Alabama on Jan. 7 in Santa Clara, California.

Lawrence replaced incumbent quarterback Kelly Bryant as the team's starter in the fifth game of the season and has embarked on a record-breaking journey since. His latest installment came on his biggest stage to date — a national semifinal at AT&T Stadium.

Lawrence completed 27 of 39 passes for 327 yards with three touchdowns, pushing his season total to 27 touchdowns against only four interceptions. It was Lawrence's fourth 300-yard passing game.

Two of the touchdown passes went to Ross, whose scoring receptions of 52 and 42 yards helped stake the Tigers to a 23-3 halftime lead. Ross set career-highs in receptions (6), receiving yards (148) and touchdown catches (2).

Sophomore wide receiver Tee Higgins had four catches for 53 yards, including a 19-yard scoring catch from Lawrence.

"Those guys are unbelievable," said Lawrence, who was named Outstanding Offensive Player of the Game. "They made a lot of plays. Just throw it in there and they'll come down with it. It makes it a lot easier on me when you have guys all around you who are great players."

The Tigers' first-half success through the air helped

With two seconds left to play in the second quarter, Clemson wide receiver Tee Higgins (5) pulls in a 19-yard touchdown past Notre Dame cornerback Donte Vaughn (8). (Ken Ruinard/Anderson Independent Mail)

open up second-half success on the ground. Running back Travis Etienne, who was held to 19 yards on seven carries in the first half, broke free for 90 yards on seven carries in the second half en route to his eighth 100-yard game of the season.

He broke Wayne Gallman's season rushing record and has 1,572 yards; he also extended his own season rushing touchdown record to 22.

Clemson's defense was dominant, holding the Fighting Irish to a season-low three points. Dexter Williams, Notre Dame's leading rusher, was held to only 54 yards. No opposing running back has rushed for more than 100 yards against Clemson since Kirvonte Benson of Georgia Tech in the eighth game of the 2017 season — a span of 19 games.

Senior defensive end Austin Bryant led a Clemson defense that amassed eight tackles for loss and six sacks

Opposite: Freshman quarterback Trevor Lawrence (16) threw for 327 yards and three touchdowns against Notre Dame on his way to earning Outstanding Offensive Player of the Game. Above: Dabo Swinney gives instruction to his team during the 30-3 Cotton Bowl victory. (Bart Boatwright/The Greenville News)

Travis Etienne high steps it into the end zone on a 62-yard touchdown carry during the third quarter. (Bart Boatwright/The Greenville News)

of Notre Dame quarterback Ian Book, who was 17 of 34 for 180 yards and an interception.

Bryant, who was named Outstanding Defensive Player of the Game, had a team-high six tackles, including three tackles for loss and two sacks as well as a quarterback hurry.

The Fighting Irish (12-1) had 248 total yards while Clemson finished with 538 yards — its seventh 500-yard game of the season.

"They were the better team today, there's no doubt about it," Notre Dame coach Brian Kelly said. "We gave up four big plays on defense, which is uncharacteristic of our defense and we generated virtually no big plays.

"Clemson was extremely smart and opportunistic and did a great job of pushing the ball vertically."

Clemson, 7-2 in its last nine bowl appearances, was making its first and only Cotton Bowl appearance since a 6-3 victory against Boston College on Jan. 1, 1940. ∎

Opposite: Clemson cornerback Trayvon Mullen (1), tight end Milan Richard (80), and running back Travis Etienne (9) are showered with confetti after being crowned Cotton Bowl champions. Above: Mullen (1) tackles Notre Dame quarterback Ian Book (12) during the first quarter. (Ken Ruinard/Anderson Independent Mail)

Wide receiver Justyn Ross (8) stiff arms Notre Dame safety Alohi Gilman (11) on the way to scoring on a 52-yard reception. (Bart Boatwright/The Greenville News)